Market Research
In A Week

Judy Bartkowiak

The Teach Yourself series has been trusted around the world for over 60 years. This series of 'In A Week' business books is designed to help people at all levels and around the world to further their careers. Learn, in a week, what the experts learn in a lifetime.

Judy Bartkowiak MA trained with Taylor Nelson in quantitative research and Bill Schlackman in qualitative research and worked with ICI Paints, Kodak and Johnson & Johnson Medical before setting up her own company, Plastow Research, in 1982. In 2000 Judy set up Kids Brands Europe (www.kids-brands.com), an agency specializing in children's market research across Europe. She has written several books, including *Secrets of Success in Brand Licensing* (2011) and *Be a happier parent with NLP* (2011) and children's fiction.

To Bill Schlackman and Liz Nelson OBE, who inspired me

Market Research

Judy Bartkowiak

www.inaweek.co.uk

Teach
Yourself®

IN A
WEEK

Hodder Education

338 Euston Road, London NW1 3BH.

Hodder Education is an Hachette UK company

First published in UK 2012 by Hodder Education

Copyright © 2012 Judy Bartkowiak

The moral rights of the author have been asserted

Database right Hodder Education (makers)

The *Teach Yourself* name is a registered trademark of Hachette UK.

British Library Cataloguing in Publication Data: a catalogue record for this title is available from the British Library.

Library of Congress Catalog Card Number: on file.

10 9 8 7 6 5 4 3 2

Hachette UK's policy is to use papers that are natural, renewable and recyclable products and made from wood grown in sustainable forests. The logging and manufacturing processes are expected to conform to the environmental regulations of the country of origin.

www.hoddereducation.co.uk

Typeset by Cenveo Publisher Services.

Printed in Great Britain by CPI Group (UK) Ltd, Croydon, CR0 4YY.

Also available in ebook

Contents

Introduction

Every day in business we make decisions. To reduce the risk associated with making these decisions, it's essential to understand your consumer and your market, and this is why we conduct market research. Decisions are not taken in a vacuum; there are competitive products and services in your marketplace, which means that consumers can choose whether or not to buy your product. Some decisions are high risk such as launching a new product, changing the packaging of an existing product, making a price change, changing the creative direction or strategy of the advertising or selling into new markets. How will your consumers react to the decisions you make and how will your competitors respond?

Whatever the size or nature of your business, you will at some point need answers to questions. To ensure you get answers that will be actionable, rather than just interesting, careful planning of the research process is crucial. The questions you have may be about who buys your product or service – your target market. We call these people 'consumers' if we are selling products and 'customers' when we are selling a service. You may also want to know about the potential target market – those people who could have a need for your product or service but currently do not know about it.

You may have questions about the market. These might relate to a geographical market or country in which you are doing business or an industry sector such as the retail market. 'Market' can also be used to describe a sector of consumers such as 'the education sector' or 'the youth market'.

In today's highly competitive and fast-moving global business environment it is ever more important to be able to anticipate consumer needs and satisfy them, because if you don't someone else surely will. Routes to market are changing and direct communication with consumers via the Internet, social media and customer loyalty programmes means that products and services can meet quite specific and niche markets more easily and cheaply than previously. Therefore accurately identifying these needs is vital.

This book takes you through the market research process from initial problem identification through research design, consideration of alternative methodologies, briefing an agency, questionnaire design and approval, to managing the project, analysis and presentation of results.

Whether you use an outside research agency or your own market research or consumer insight department, spending a week to understand the process will give you unique skills which will ensure that you get the research results you need that will address the marketing questions you have. Market research is a fascinating marketing tool and it is not unusual to find that, once you have decided to conduct research, everyone in your organization wants to add their own marketing issues. 'Can we just ask...?', 'It's only one more question...' are what you'll hear. Unless you take control, you can end up with research results that answer none of them, including your own. Designing one project to fulfil very different needs can be more expensive than several separate, smaller-scale projects designed to meet their specific objectives. This book will help you design different types of survey.

This week you will gain a basic understanding of market research without the jargon or the detail that you would need as a research supplier. It will enable you to commission market research, as a client or user of research. It will be invaluable to you if you are a student of marketing and want a quick guide to conducting research for your dissertation. It will also be useful to junior researchers who want an overview of the whole process or an easy reference guide.

Judy Bartkowiak

SUNDAY

Market research and project design

Market research is a vital tool for growing a business. Our business decisions must be based on understanding consumers and the competitive environment, remembering that consumers have choice. We need to ask questions that are pertinent to the decisions we must make and design surveys that answer these questions, which means taking careful ownership of them so they achieve what we intended.

Today we will start with a brief overview of what market research is and how it can provide the information you need to grow your business. You will learn about 'the marketing mix', market segmentation, different uses for and types of market research, and the questions to ask before you embark on a research project. You will then learn how to design a survey that meets your objectives, by considering the purpose of your research and how to use it to reduce the risk of making ill-informed marketing decisions.

The UK Market Research Society says:

'Market Research is one of the most useful tools in business, the way in which organizations find out about what their customers and potential customers need, want and care about.'

What is market research?

The American Marketing Association (AMA) defines market research as:

'the function which links the consumer, customer, and the public to the marketer through information – information used to identify and define marketing opportunities and problems; generate, refine and evaluate marketing actions; monitor marketing performance; and improve understanding of marketing as a process. Market research specifies the information required to address these issues; designs the method for collecting information; manages and implements the data collection process; analyses the results and communicates the findings and their implications.'

The UK Market Research Society emphasizes that market research is the conduit between the marketer and the consumer. Nowadays the term 'consumer insight' tends to be used slightly more than market research, to reflect the growing importance of proactively seeking insight and knowledge about consumers rather than simply reporting data.

It's important to understand that market research is *never* about selling. You may have had phone calls or even been approached in the street by so-called 'researchers' conducting surveys under the guise of market research, when in fact they want to sell you something.

The marketing mix

Market research is a marketing tool used across the entire marketing function, which is called the marketing mix. The marketing mix describes the four aspects of marketing: product, price, promotion and place (the four Ps).

It is essentially the consumers' *perception* of product, price, promotion and place that is key, and this is where market research is required.

Product

This includes all aspects of the product itself, the product range and all variants of the product. Typical product-related research could cover any of the following:

- customer need of this product or service
- features and physical attributes such as size, shape, colour, functionality, taste, smell
- brand imagery and associations
- usage – how the product or service is used
- attitudes – how consumers relate to it
- product name and branding
- packaging
- competitive positioning
- sales and market share.

Price

This is everything associated with the pricing strategy of a product, which will vary according to how desirable your brand is perceived to be over the competitor's. There will always be a limit on price within any product category, although this will be much higher if you can present a highly differentiated, unique product, offering a benefit on which consumers place high value.

Price-related research addresses the following types of issue:

- the value of the product or service to the buyer
- established price points in this market
- how price sensitive the market is and how it responds to small changes in price
- whether to offer discounts
- perceived price/value perceptions versus those of competitors.

Promotion

Promotion covers everything to do with how a product is promoted, and includes sponsorship, public relations and live events as well as advertising. Viral marketing is becoming increasingly important for promotion, especially via social network sites such as Facebook and Twitter. Effective promotions involve delivering the right message to the right messengers in the right environment. The message itself needs to be memorable and relevant.

Promotions-related research will cover:

- how the target market consumes advertising media
- the best time to promote, taking account of any seasonality in the market
- how your competitors do their promotions and how that influences your choice of promotional activity
- promotion awareness and recall
- comprehension, credibility and relevance of the communication
- response to the creative execution of the promotion
- potential sponsorship opportunities.

Place

Place refers to the channels of distribution, i.e. where the product is sold. This might be in shops, online or both. Research in this area may focus on some of these issues:

- where buyers expect to find your product or service
- sales process, e.g. sales force, catalogue, website, trade shows

- what your competitors do, and how you can learn from this and differentiate
- how consumers will access your customer service and how problems will be resolved.

> **'Marketing is the management process responsible for identifying, anticipating and satisfying customer requirements profitably.'**
>
> Chartered Institute of Marketing

Segmenting your market

Fundamental to marketing is the practice of segmenting the market. This means dividing consumers into groups, where consumers within one group have similar needs that are different from those in other groups.

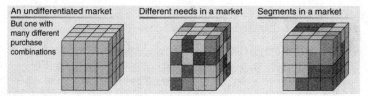

Market segments © Professor Malcolm McDonald

These different consumer groups will require a different marketing strategy, which means that – from the market research perspective – surveys will usually focus on a specific segment or be analysed by segments in order for the findings to be actionable for the marketer. This will be because each segment will have different needs, competitive set, cultural values, advertising exposure and so on.

Segments may be defined by:

- demographics, e.g. age, life stage, socio-economic group
- geographical area, e.g. Europe, the Middle East, Asia, the US
- the maturity of the market
- industry or market sector.

When planning your market research survey, it is important to identify your segments to ensure that you can interpret the results and action them according to explicit consumer needs. Different segments lend themselves to different research methodology, in terms of both what is possible and what is most suitable. Mostly this will be obvious. You wouldn't, for example, conduct a quantitative survey about a new software package on the street with businessmen.

If your market is not segmented at this point, you can tackle this at the analysis stage of a large-scale survey by requesting cluster analysis from your research supplier. This will programme the data in such a way as to draw out the segments for you.

Full knowledge will reduce the risk associated with making decisions about launching new products or entering new markets. Accurate predictions about future sales and pricing strategies will ensure that you have sufficient stock and that it will sell at the best price.

The 80:20 rule

In most businesses the 80:20 rule applies, whereby 20 per cent of your customers or consumers account for 80 per cent of sales. We refer to them as our **core target market**. If you work in a small company operating on a business-to-business (B2B) basis, you may even know these customers by name and speak to them weekly. In these circumstances it will be easier to ask them about a new product or service you are considering introducing and, indeed, they may be the instigators of an innovation.

In a business-to-consumer (B2C) company, the 20 per cent who regularly buy your product may be defined by demographics such as age, life stage or socio-economic group or by psychographics such as personality type. In some cases they may be defined by media consumption, such as what papers or magazines they read and what TV programmes they watch. In other cases people may have a particular hobby or interest that might define them as your customers, such as going on cruises or running.

The uses of market research

Here are some of the many uses of market research:

- to identify marketing opportunities for new products
- to measure market share, brand awareness, advertising awareness and competitive position
- to identify, anticipate and satisfy consumer and customer requirements, attitudes and behaviour in relation to a product or service in all areas of the marketing mix: product, price, promotion and place (channels of distribution)
- to assess brand imagery and USP (unique selling proposition)
- to segment the market to enable products and services to be designed to meet the needs of different types of customer
- to reduce the risk of making strategic or operational decisions without evidence.

The more knowledge you have of your consumers and your market, the more accurately you will target them with the relevant communication and products, which in turn will lead to higher profits.

Types of market research

Market research covers a wide range of activities. The list below shows the variety of surveys that can be done. Each provides a different type of insight, and at the design stage it is useful to be aware of them all.

- **'Comp' shops** – looking at what the competitors are doing by going into their shops or trying out their brands, checking out their website, observing their events and so on.
- **Mystery shopping** – conducting a survey where you employ interviewers to behave as customers and report back to you about customer service, product experience and so on.
- **Omnibus surveys** – placing your own questions on a large-scale survey managed by a research agency. You receive the results of your own questions only. It is a cost-effective way to collect data.

SUNDAY

MONDAY

TUESDAY

WEDNESDAY

THURSDAY

FRIDAY

SATURDAY

- **Panels** – often comprising your own customers or consumers, who agree to complete a questionnaire on a regular basis in return for a fee or vouchers. These are particularly useful if you have a target market that is difficult to find by conventional means, such as readers of a particular magazine.
- **Ad hoc surveys** – surveys designed to address a specific area of investigation in specific countries or areas with specific target groups. They can be qualitative or quantitative.
- **Tracking or continuous surveys** – surveys conducted at regular intervals to monitor changes in any aspect of your marketing mix.
- **Accompanied shopping** – when the interviewer accompanies the consumer as they do their shop, noting their behaviour and asking them about it, recording the interview.
- **Ethnography** – when the interviewer spends time in the consumer's home, observes how they interact with the product and gathers insights about their lifestyle, attitudes and behaviour.

On Tuesday and Wednesday you will learn about all these in more detail.

Before you start your research

Communication within organizations is never perfect, so before you embark on an expensive research project there are several questions to ask yourself first.

- Is this a real marketing issue or simply political posturing within my organization to make a point, explain poor performance or further someone's career?
- Has the question I am asking or the information required already been addressed elsewhere? If it has can that information be used for my purposes? Could the data that exists be interrogated or analysed in another way to give me what I need?
- Are there surveys already in place or planned to which I could add my questions?

- Could the cost of the survey be shared with another department that has similar issues, or the same target consumer or customer or area of interest?
- Can the decision wait until survey results are available? Has the decision already been taken?
- Do I have access to any online facility whereby I could access consumers quickly and cheaply?
- Can someone internally answer my question, such as the salespeople who have regular contact with customers, retail or industry?
- Can the data be provided more cheaply using secondary research?

Primary and secondary research

There are two types of research: primary and secondary. **Primary research** is the research we will be covering in this book and relates to research we conduct ourselves, directly with the consumer or customer, for our own purpose and use. It can be:

- ad hoc – in that we conduct the research to focus on a specific information need at the point we need it
- continuous – where we regularly conduct a survey in order to track specific information about our customers or our market, such as pricing, distribution, customer satisfaction, awareness, sales, usage and attitudes (U&A) and brand associations.

Secondary research uses data that already exists. It may be data you already have from past surveys, customer service records, barcode information, loyalty card records, databases, your website or other internal information you hold about your customers. It also includes research done on the Internet, surveys held in business libraries such as the CIM (Chartered Institute of Marketing) and the products of the many companies that regularly provide research reports to which you can subscribe, such as Mintel (www.mintel.com), which provides global intelligence for every product sector on a regular basis. Nielsen (www.nielsen.com) provides worldwide data on what consumers buy and watch. For a full list of companies providing research services, consult ESOMAR (the European Society for Opinion and Market Research www.esomar.org), where you can also find out about market research conferences, publications and codes of conduct.

Check before commissioning primary research that what you want isn't already available internally or through one of the many large market research agencies. These providers dictate the objectives of secondary research and you simply buy their data, although in many cases you can specify how you want the results analysed and reported. By contrast, primary research is fully controlled by you, the client. This means that you need to be absolutely clear about how the research will be used before you begin to design your survey.

What is the purpose of the research?

The first question to ask is, **'What decision will I take based on this research?'**

Market research, especially quantitative research, which provides numbers essentially, should start from a hypothesis. The **null hypothesis (H0)** is usually the least likely outcome of the research, such as 'The new packaging format will make no difference to existing customers; their propensity to purchase will be the same as for the existing packaging format.' Clearly, the new packaging format is being considered in order to increase propensity to purchase, so if it doesn't increase, it would be a costly decision to change it.

The **alternative hypothesis (H1)** might be 'The new packaging format will appeal to potential purchasers who currently buy competitive brands, and the new format will increase their propensity to purchase our brand in preference.'

Both hypotheses show what the research needs to test.

- The null hypothesis relates to 'no change' among existing customers.
- The alternative hypothesis relates to an increased propensity to purchase among potential customers.

However, what level of increased propensity to purchase will warrant the expense of a new packaging format? This needs to be decided in advance of designing the research because it will affect the sample needed for statistical accuracy.

Also, is it propensity to purchase that is the key decider or could it be communication of brand values? The likelihood is that both are important. Again, hypotheses need to be generated; for example 'The new packaging format will communicate *ease of use* more effectively than the existing packaging format.'

Quantitative or qualitative?

Do you need insight or solid statistics? In the above examples relating to hypotheses, quantitative research would be indicated, but companies also need insight from qualitative research regarding understanding how their brand is perceived, what part it plays in consumers' lives, what it says about them when they use the product, what other types of product this brand could develop and so on. More on this tomorrow! For now, think about what evidence you need from your research in order to make your marketing decision. What needs to be true for you to make this decision?

It can be useful to project forward to the results of your survey and write down a list of what you would need to see in the research report in order to know that you can make a decision confidently. Research results are always fascinating, and it is easy to get caught up in the detail and delight in the increased knowledge about your consumers and the market. However, research is costly and time-consuming. It has to serve the end purpose of being a marketing tool. It may help to go through the SMART goals shown below.

SMART goals

Set out your SMART goals at the research design stage.

Specific – whether the research is largely fact finding or a regular tracking survey, exploratory or creative, every question – be it on a quantitative questionnaire or on a qualitative topic guide – needs to be there for a specific reason that is agreed with all parties to the research.

Measurable – whether you measure by quantitative means or qualitative, it must still be possible to measure the results in terms of either the hypotheses you set up for the quantitative or the insight you require in the qualitative. Qualitative is often measured by the richness of the insight, the 'nuggets' ('aha' moments) or new ideas.

Achievable – the sample needs to be achievable, in terms of being able to find the right people and persuade them to be interviewed.

Realistic – are the questions relevant to the sample, is it realistic that they will have an opinion on the subject and will they care enough to spend their time answering questions about it?

Timely – when do you need results? If the survey is to be done in several countries, has a large sample size or involves extensive coding of open-ended questions, you will need to factor this into the design.

Finally, you'll need to decide who is taking ownership of this survey. Your first step is to write the market research brief, which we will do tomorrow.

Summary

Today you learned that market research is a tool used to identify and define marketing opportunities, linking the consumer with the marketer whose function it is to satisfy consumer needs at a profit. Marketing comprises the four Ps: product, price, promotion and place. Market research can tell us about any or all of these areas so that we can make decisions, confident that consumers will respond favourably to them.

Markets are segmented by factors that combine similar types of consumer with similar needs, which are different from those of other segments. By this process, marketing can direct its efforts appropriately. These segments will also determine how the market research will be conducted and which groups will be surveyed according to the nature of the survey.

You learned that you need to ask a number of questions before embarking on research, and that secondary data may be available that will avoid the requirement for more expensive primary research. By carefully defining the purpose of your research and applying SMART goals, you can make sure that your market research will get off to the best start possible.

SUNDAY
MONDAY
TUESDAY
WEDNESDAY
THURSDAY
FRIDAY
SATURDAY

Fact-check (answers at the back)

1. Whose needs are we aiming to understand in a market research survey?
   a) The marketing department's ❏
   b) The managing director's ❏
   c) The consumer's ❏
   d) The market research agency's ❏

2. What are the four Ps?
   a) People, price, promotion, place ❏
   b) Product, price, promotion, place ❏
   c) Product, packaging, promotion, place ❏
   d) Packaging, personnel, price, promotion ❏

3. What is the most important consideration when designing a survey?
   a) What decision will be taken based on the results ❏
   b) How much it will cost ❏
   c) Who will conduct the research ❏
   d) How long it will take ❏

4. What is an omnibus survey?
   a) A survey of people on a bus ❏
   b) A large-scale survey of your customers ❏
   c) A survey to which you can add your own questions ❏
   d) A survey that anyone can answer ❏

5. What is segmentation?
   a) Groups of consumers who are all similar to each other ❏
   b) Groups of consumers who are similar to each other and different from other groups ❏
   c) Groups of consumers who are different from each other ❏
   d) Groups of consumers who like each other ❏

6. What is primary research?
   a) Research conducted by the client to satisfy their specific information needs ❏
   b) Research you conduct first ❏
   c) Very expensive research ❏
   d) Research of your own internal resources ❏

7. What is B2B?
   a) Business to consumer ❏
   b) Business to Benelux ❏
   c) Business to business ❏
   d) Business to baby ❏

8. What is price sensitivity?
   a) How consumers respond to a high price ❏
   b) How consumers respond to a low price ❏
   c) How consumers respond to a change in price ❏
   d) How consumers respond to special offers ❏

9. What are social media?
   a) Friendly customers ❏
   b) Magazines ❏
   c) Nightclubs ❏
   d) Twitter, Facebook, LinkedIn ❏

10. Where can you find out about the services of secondary data providers?
a) ESOMAR and the Market Research Society ☐
b) CIM ☐
c) Nielsen ☐
d) Mintel ☐

MONDAY

The research brief and research proposal

Now that you have considered the purpose and importance of research in informing the marketing decisions you need to take, you can embark on your market research project.

Today we will look at the first stage in your project, which is writing the research brief and preparing the research proposal. If you are commissioning research from an outside agency, you will need to find out which agencies have the expertise you need, in both the product category and the research methodology you anticipate using. You ask these suppliers to submit proposals, which you then review and decide who you would like to invite to discuss the project further.

The research brief is an important process because it is the first time you 'go public' with your project and make it a reality. Today you will learn what information you need to provide in your brief in order to receive, in response, a proposal that meets your marketing needs.

The research proposal is the document that effectively forms a contract between client and supplier. It itemizes what will happen in the project and what you will get for your money.

The market research brief

Once you have decided to conduct market research and have established the purpose of the survey, a brief needs to be written. The process of writing a brief is a rigorous one and requires understanding of every element of the marketing mix.

There will be a number of stakeholders involved from different departments in your organization and all will need to be consulted in order to check that the research will cover what they need to know in order to make their decisions. It is from them that you will acquire the information you need to write the research brief.

Expect it to be a document of a few pages, possibly with appendices, which may include findings from previous projects that you want the supplier to read so that they inform their proposal. If you already know the suppliers, this stage could be covered by a telephone conversation or an email. The supplier will need to know what you want them to include in the proposal, and they may need further information from you that you will then need to add to the brief.

Send the brief to suppliers who you know are experts in this field of research, companies known to you with whom you have worked in the past or who have been recommended. Contact each supplier before sending them the brief, to check that they are able to provide you with a proposal and to find out to whom specifically you should send it. It is usual to send out the brief to about three suppliers and to give them a week to respond.

Key components of the brief are as follows.

1 Background
2 Marketing objectives
3 Research objectives
4 The sample
5 Methodology
6 Timing
7 Budget
8 The presentation and report
9 Format and timing for proposals
10 Contact details

1 Background

Research projects are often commandeered by every department in an organization and, like a ship without a hand on the tiller, your project can head off in any one of a number of different directions if you don't anchor the project with a clear focus on what triggered the decision to research in the first place. The trigger factor may have already become a little lost by the time you start writing the brief, so you may need to look back at the notes of the first meeting and speak again with the parties who instigated the project.

What triggered the research and why does it need to be done now?

When commissioning market research from an agency, it is important to give the agency as much information as possible. It may be tempting to hold back on political issues, diverging corporate views and other contentious matters but unless the agency is fully in the picture, they cannot do the best job for you. The agency should be working 'with you' rather than 'for you' as part of your marketing team.

Background information should include:

● company brand and product portfolio
● corporate mission statement

- brand or product history and past research findings that could relate to this project
- share of the market now and historically
- detailed information about your consumers and purchasers, e.g. what type of people they are and why they buy this product or service
- brand awareness – spontaneous and prompted
- brand personality
- channels of distribution
- pricing structure
- competitive brands.

It is also important to send them samples of the product and competitive products so that they can familiarize themselves with them as they write the proposal. Physically feeling, consuming and using the product gives insight much needed at this stage of the project. They will undoubtedly refer to your website for information, so send them the link and highlight the sections of the website that will be most useful.

If the supplier has previously conducted research for you on this brand, you can reduce the amount of content in the background section and just focus on what is current now and what has triggered the need for research. For new suppliers, the background needs to be thorough to prevent them including in their proposal issues that have already been researched and to ensure that they base this proposal only on what you need to know now.

Supply relevant past research findings at the briefing stage so that the lessons learned can inform this next project and prevent it repeating surveys already carried out and which haven't changed.

2 Marketing objectives

The research agency needs to know what actions or decisions will be taken based on their research findings.

In most cases you will already have an idea of what results to expect because you are familiar with the brand. Qualitative research may already have been conducted on the concept and this survey may be designed to provide quantitative findings. So what is the hypothesis that they need to test? A typical hypothesis for a new product development project would be that there is a market for the new product. You need to know the potential size of it and the likely consumer profile, to ensure it adds market share rather than takes away from it.

It is usual to provide one main marketing objective, which may be overarching such as, 'To determine whether there is a market among existing customers for a new flavour of coffee based on neutraceutical benefits such as reducing blood pressure'.

Secondary marketing objectives will almost certainly be needed in order to make the marketing decision based on this research. They could be:

- how likely customers will be to buy the new flavour
- whether it will be instead of their current flavour or in addition
- how much more they will pay for the medical benefit
- whether they believe the medical benefit
- what other medical benefits would appeal.

It needs to be clear from the marketing objectives what level of accuracy you need. For example, is it insight or figures? Based on the main objectives, a supplier might be inclined to recommend qualitative research to explore the appeal of the concept of this new flavour, but the secondary objectives indicate that the research will need to be quantified: for example, 'how likely...to buy' indicates that a propensity to purchase question will be needed and 'how much...' indicates a price sensitivity question. You'd find both of these in a quantitative questionnaire.

The segments in which you want to research need to be specified so that the research supplier can estimate the size of the sample needed, how easy they will be to find and what type of people they will be. In the above example we know that it is existing customers of the brand who are to be sampled.

The brief should tell the research supplier as much as possible about their customers in terms of age, life stage and socio-economic group, whether they are more prevalent in certain countries, in the north or south of the country, working or non-working and where they tend to shop.

3 Research objectives

Although there may be some overlap between the marketing objectives and the research objectives, expect to spend more time articulating the research objectives as they will determine what methodology the supplier will advocate to meet them. The research objectives will therefore be more detailed and specific. They will usually be a list of information needs, which could almost be a questionnaire in itself. It is, in effect, a list of what you want to know and whether you want insight or to measure this factor.

Taking the example above (coffee), the research objectives might be:

- What is the response to new coffee concepts (three different concepts)?
  - Do existing customers of Brand X respond favourably?
  - Do people with high blood pressure respond more favourably?
  - Is it credible?
  - Is it relevant?
  - Is it understandable?
  - What are the taste expectations?
  - What are the cost expectations?
  - What are the drinking occasions?
  - What is the interest in other 'medical' claims?
  - What other products offer this claim?
- What are current associations between coffee and blood pressure?
- What is the level of understanding of high blood pressure and its causes?
- How likely would consumers be to buy it?
  - Would they buy it instead of the current flavour or as well?
  - How much more would they pay for it?
  - Where would they expect to see it?

This list is by no means exhaustive, but it serves as an example to show that more detail needs to be in the research objectives section of the brief.

4 The sample

The 'sample' refers to who will be interviewed. On Sunday you learned about segmentation because you need to know which segments will be targeted in the research and how you define them. For example, if you know that one type of customer tends to respond differently to another and that both types of customer are relevant to this research study, they need to be described fully so that the supplier can identify them and understand the differences. If age is significant, you should specify the age breaks (age bands) in which you usually

SUNDAY

MONDAY

TUESDAY

WEDNESDAY

THURSDAY

FRIDAY

SATURDAY

analyse data. Many clients like to tie these in with age bands used in their continuous or tracking research.

Research suppliers will expect information about whether this survey is to be single country or multi-country and who will qualify for inclusion. Again, areas may need to be specified if you usually split countries in a particular way or analyse by TV region, retail areas, sales areas and so on.

If the sample is users of a particular product or brand, the brand share needs to be specified here so that the research supplier can estimate the 'hit rate' for interviewers. In other words, if they are interviewing on the street, they need to know how many people they will need to approach before finding someone who qualifies for interview.

If it will be hard to find the sample, you will need to suggest where they can be found more easily. 'Special interest groups' could be accessible online or in clubs, retail outlets and other areas where your brand share is strong. If the sample is to be people who have heard of the brand, you will need to supply spontaneous and prompted awareness figures and information about where awareness is highest and how these people can be found.

In the coffee example, the research objectives would indicate a qualitative stage, so it would be relevant to specify focus groups that include people who suffer from high blood pressure. Figures and the profile for this sample should be given here.

5 Methodology

You may prefer to leave the choice of methodology up to the agency, even if you have an idea of what you are expecting. This way you have 'fresh thinking' on the project and an opportunity to challenge what you had thought would be the methodology. Competing suppliers may have suggested different methodologies in their proposals, and that can give you a chance to consider options and select what best meets your timing and cost constraints as well as the research objectives.

If you have your own market research or consumer insight department, you may be sufficiently experienced to specify the methodology to be used. It is then up to the research agency to go with this suggestion or recommend something different.

Make it clear in your brief whether you are open to suggestions or whether the methodology is already decided.

6 Timing

You know when your marketing department needs to make the decision, and you will need the results of the research in sufficient time to allow you to interpret the findings and present them internally, with your recommendations. Make sure your research suppliers are clear about when you need them to be presenting the findings to you. You may want to specify one date for a verbal debrief (presentation) of the findings and another for the final report, because in most cases marketing decisions will be taken based on the presentation and justified later by the report.

7 Budget

The amount of money available for the project needs to be specified here. Don't be tempted to exclude this section because you believe that the research agency will simply spend all of it. This is probably true but, by not mentioning it, the chances are that you will not get the best research design. The reason for this is that agencies will avoid the costliest approaches, which may in fact be what are needed. Also, agencies you haven't worked with before will have no idea what to suggest and, because they want the work, they may underestimate how much the research will cost, especially if yours is a 'hard-to-find' sample. They will then cut corners elsewhere to keep within budget.

While you may be reluctant to give the agency an idea of budget in the belief that they'll spend the maximum for you, this is counterproductive. Quantitative research is significantly more expensive than qualitative, so if your research objectives indicate quantitative, for example brand awareness, they will have to do this quantitatively. You will therefore get a high quote when perhaps brand awareness was not a key objective.

Other clients simply don't know how much the research is likely to cost and therefore don't include it. The problem here is that the agency then has no idea how ambitious it can be. Most agencies, on reading the brief, will know what to recommend, especially if they have researched for this client before, but unless they know what the budget is they will be reluctant to specify an ambitious research design for fear of not getting the project.

A compromise option is to indicate a range of budgets, starting from what you suspect it will cost to what you could afford for a top-class research design covering everything you want, and more.

> **TIP** If the cost of the project is to be shared across different departments or country offices, ask for the costs to be split or allocated in whatever way will clearly show this best for your stakeholders.

8 The presentation and report

Research suppliers expect to be told how they will need to deliver their research findings. They will want to know whether they must make a presentation and, if so, where it will be and who will be attending, what facilities there will be, whether it will be by video conference and how long they will be given. If a number of stakeholders want to attend, it is usual to specify the date of the presentation in the briefing document.

You should also tell the suppliers the format required for their report, which will be covered in detail on Saturday. It is common practice to give a copy of the presentation to clients and a more detailed report containing summary tables and the data tables for reference, as well as a report with detailed coverage of all the points mentioned in the research objectives. A management summary is often required as well, for stakeholders who have a more peripheral involvement in the project.

9 Format and timing for proposals

Research suppliers need to know when you expect to receive a copy of the proposal, how many copies are needed and in what format. You should specify whom they need to send the proposal to and their contact details. Allow suppliers at least a week to consider their response to your brief.

10 Contact details

You should add your own contact details for them to use should they have any questions about the brief.

The market research proposal

It is the job of a research supplier or agency to respond to a brief by considering the requirements, familiarizing themselves with the product and product category and any previous research findings supplied, and provide a written proposal. The research buyer appraises and compares all the proposals submitted to decide which one best meets their brief.

The chosen proposal becomes in effect the contract between the client and the supplier, committing the parties to a specific research design with agreed timings and costs. It is therefore vital that everything that needs to be included is there for both to refer to. The research proposal should include the following key components.

1 Background
2 Objectives
3 Methodology
4 Reporting and presentation
5 Timing

6 Cost
7 Stimulus materials
8 Terms of business
9 Credentials

1 Background

This section should be a response to the brief, confirming that the marketing objectives have been understood and the background supplied by the client has been considered. Other work in this product category may be alluded to and general observations made about it, although research findings belonging to another client should not be included. Research buyers are usually impressed when they see that an agency has information or insight in addition to what they have provided.

2 Objectives

In the research objectives section it is usual to use words that show specifically that the supplier understands the brief in terms of whether it will require quantitative or qualitative research, or both. Expect to see words like:

- to explore (qualitative)
- to identify (qualitative)
- to investigate (qualitative)
- to measure (quantitative)
- to determine (quantitative)
- to quantify (quantitative).

In most cases research proposals offer a main objective and possibly two or three secondary objectives. It is not usual to list questions at this stage and, if there were questions in the brief, they will have been grouped into specific objectives for the purposes of the proposal.

3 Methodology

This is arguably the most important section of the proposal, as it is where the supplier shows how the research methodology chosen will address different aspects of the brief. This section needs to cover not only methodology chosen but also suggested stages, such as qualitative and then quantitative. The agency needs to justify the choice of research method, what it will provide, how it will meet the research objectives and what exactly it will involve.

The proposal does not need to include a questionnaire or group topic guide at this stage, but it is usual to show which research objectives will be covered by each methodology chosen so that the buyer can check that each has been covered.

If the research is qualitative, expect to see information about:

- number of focus groups
- recruitment criteria
- where the sessions will take place
- how long they will be
- stimuli to be shown.

Quantitative research needs to include:

- exclusion categories
- databases to be used for recruitment (if relevant)
- sample size and statistical significance (more on this on Friday)
- sampling points (towns or cities where the research will be conducted)
- sample details, number of respondents in each cell, demographics and usage criteria
- stimuli to be shown
- questionnaire length
- analysis tools.

... AS SOMEONE WHO FITS OUR TYPICAL CUSTOMER PROFILE, ...

4 Report and presentation

The research supplier will confirm the reporting and presentation required by the briefing document as well as any progress reports that might be beneficial, especially during complicated multi-country projects.

5 Timing

This section needs to impress the buyer in terms of meeting their deadlines but must also be realistic and achievable. Clear timelines need to be outlined on a week-by-week basis, so that the client can check that they can provide what the agency needs in terms of stimuli in time for fieldwork (interviewing). Draft questionnaires for quantitative projects often have to be agreed internally by several stakeholders, translated and agreed internationally for multi-country projects and then piloted before final versions are available for research. This process can take weeks.

6 Cost

This section outlines the cost, broken down into sections so the client can see what costs apply to different stages or countries, enabling costs to be allocated to different country budgets if necessary. If a budget range was provided by the brief, this may indicate that the client wants to have options to add stages, countries or adjust the sample size. A full breakdown enables them to do this.

The currency of the supplier may not be the same as the client's, so it needs to be clear what exchange rate is being used and in what currency the supplier wants to be paid.

7 Stimulus materials

Most projects need stimulus material. In qualitative projects this could include concept boards, mood boards, products, advertising and point-of-sale materials. Quantitative projects usually require minimal stimuli, but interviewers often show examples of pack design, logos, concept statements and cards depicting competitive products. These need to be prepared, so the proposal should clearly describe what stimuli are needed, as well as details of number of copies, timings for their production and how they need to be approved.

8 Terms of business

The agency will specify their terms of business, which is usually 25–50 per cent on commission payable within 60–90 days. This is to cover costs that will be incurred well before the project is complete, such as paying interviewers weekly. The remaining costs are usually invoiced on completion, but this needs to be specified in this section.

9 Credentials

Here you will find a list of the people who will be working on your project, along with their CVs or professional background and experience. This enables you to verify that they have the strengths you need for the project team. You will also find details about the clients they have worked for and whether they have experience in this specific market. In addition, the company credentials will appear here, with its experience in the product category and market.

This section may also include references from clients to demonstrate their ability to handle your project successfully.

Check that your market research agency is a member of the MRS (the Market Research Society), ESOMAR (the European Society for Opinion and Market Research) or CASRO (the Council of American Survey Research Organizations), as this ensures that they are complying with quality and legal requirements and that they are professionally qualified.

The project begins

Once the agency has been selected and costs and timings agreed, you will need to have a meeting to brief the agency more fully on your project. You should insist that the moderator or researcher conducting the project be at this meeting.

Once the project begins, the agency will keep you informed on progress. You can attend fieldwork and encourage your team to do so too. Increasingly, clients are involved in the focus groups and will be asked at the end whether they have any specific questions not already covered.

For quantitative surveys, there will probably be several drafts of the questionnaire for each market and sometimes this can result in mistakes and typos being missed as client teams concentrate on content. It is therefore important that the agency pilot it (test it out on a small sample first) before fieldwork starts, to ensure that any errors are picked up.

Before the first day of fieldwork – whether qualitative or quantitative – it is your responsibility to ensure that your team is fully briefed on what is taking place and given the opportunity to add any issues they feel have been omitted from the checklist agreed between you and the agency.

Summary

The research brief and research proposal are crucial to the success of any market research project because they set out the client's needs and the supplier's response. Both documents will be referred to throughout the project and should be adhered to. Each document should have the detail and structure needed to fulfil the objectives and provide the basis for everyone working on it. This requires a great deal of time to prepare and consider all eventualities, so that nothing is left to chance.

The two documents will have many common elements, in that the proposal reflects back to the buyer what they have provided by way of background. The supplier will expand on each section, though, with their own ideas and experience in that market or the product category. Once the project is commissioned, the proposal becomes a legally binding contract that both sides will work to throughout the project.

SUNDAY
MONDAY
TUESDAY
WEDNESDAY
THURSDAY
FRIDAY
SATURDAY

Fact-check (answers at the back)

1. Who should you send your research brief to?
   a) Research agencies you've worked with in the past ❑
   b) Research agencies you've heard of ❑
   c) Research agencies that colleagues have recommended ❑
   d) Research agencies with the expertise you need ❑

2. What should background information include?
   a) As little as possible, so they have to do all the work ❑
   b) All relevant information about the company, product and your consumers ❑
   c) As much as you have time to write ❑
   d) Nothing that could be confidential information ❑

3. Why are the marketing objectives important?
   a) The research is there to serve marketing as a tool for decision making ❑
   b) They keep the marketing department happy ❑
   c) They serve as a check that the research objectives meet them ❑
   d) They keep the focus on how the research will be used ❑

4. What are the research objectives?
   a) The issues and questions the research needs to answer ❑
   b) How to find the answers to the marketing objectives ❑
   c) What the research supplier needs to include in the proposal ❑
   d) A list of questions to include in the questionnaire ❑

5. Why do you need to include the research budget in the brief?
   a) So that the agency knows how much to charge ❑
   b) Because it is a legal requirement ❑
   c) Because it shows you value research ❑
   d) So that the agency knows the maximum it can charge ❑

6. How much time should you give an agency to respond with a proposal?
   a) As much time as they want ❑
   b) About a week, to allow them time to consider the brief ❑
   c) A day or two ❑
   d) It depends on the complexity of the brief ❑

7. Does an agency need to include the questionnaire in the proposal?
a) Yes, because the client wants to see what it would look like ☐
b) No; that will be done after the briefing meeting ☐
c) No; that will be done after the project is commissioned ☐
d) Yes, because it will impress the client ☐

8. How detailed should the costing be?
a) Just a ballpark figure because it may change ☐
b) Every single cost should be included ☐
c) Separate costs for each stage ☐
d) Refer to the brief ☐

9. What should be in the credentials section?
a) Contact details ☐
b) Company details ☐
c) The experience and qualifications of everyone working on the project ☐
d) Company references ☐

10. Why is it important to allow plenty of time to design the questionnaire?
a) It needs to be piloted ☐
b) All the stakeholders need to approve it ☐
c) It may need to be translated ☐
d) All of the above ☐

TUESDAY

Qualitative market research

Market research methods may be ongoing or ad hoc, qualitative or quantitative, single country or multi-country, online or offline. However do you choose? The most significant decision for most issues is whether to choose qualitative or quantitative, although some methodologies may to some extent combine the two.

Today you will learn about the different types of qualitative market research. Developed in the 1950s and called motivational research, this term typifies how qualitative research is still used today. It gets under the consumer's conscious behaviour and rational response to understand their inner motivations regarding the brand in question.

There are many methodologies to choose from, and you do not have to choose just one. It is quite usual to conduct different pieces of research to cover different aspects of the issue you want to address. Usually they are conducted sequentially so that the learning from one can lead neatly into the next, enabling you to refine your questions, direct your sampling and build the learning about your consumers so that your research is cost-effective and produces results you can action.

When to use qualitative research

As you read through the different descriptions you may find that there are aspects of several that seem to fit the bill. Because of this, the depth interviewer or focus group moderator needs specific skills.

Qualitative research is the most appropriate option in situations when we need insight, understanding and the opportunity for respondents to tell us what is important to them, rather than us giving them options via a questionnaire. Typically, qualitative research is:

- unstructured, in that it uses a topic guide that lists areas for discussion or topics rather than questions
- done with small samples and not meant to be representative statistically
- focused on *why* consumers do what they do, *why* they perceive what they perceive and not on *what* they do.

It is used in the exploratory stage of a research project. In some cases this may be the only stage, but more often it is the first stage in a project that will move on to a quantitative stage based on the findings of the qualitative work. The aims of qualitative research may be:

- to explore terminology used within a market that is new either in terms of product category or segment, to find out:
  - how consumers refer to the product
  - how they describe it
  - what words this segment uses
- to help define a problem, e.g. if sales are falling and you want to explore the possible reasons before quantifying them. The research will provide the list of pre-codes (answers on the questionnaire) for respondents to choose from
- to reduce the number of options prior to quantifying, e.g. if you have ten possible flavours of ice cream, you may want to eliminate the least appealing to focus on the most popular ones in a quantitative survey
- to identify new product concepts, new uses for a product, new channels of distribution, such as:

- perceived strengths and weaknesses of the new concept
- potential target market for the new concept
- improvements and developments of the new concept

● to understand how the advertising communication or pack design is working through the following steps:
  - show alternative executions at mock-up stage
  - initial reactions, strengths and weaknesses of each
  - eliminate those that are rejected
  - detailed response to artwork – font, copy, colours, illustrations, logo, message
  - detailed response to advertising creative – voice, tone, storyline, music, message, characters

● to understand how your consumers use your product or service and what part it plays in their lives, by asking:
  - what other options they consider
  - how they feel about it at a deeper level
  - what buying this brand says about them as a person.

Payments

In most cases a financial or other incentive will be offered to respondents. Gift vouchers for the product are a common payment method, and charity vouchers may also be offered, if appropriate.

Consumers buy brands they feel a connection with. Qualitative research enables us to share this connection with respondents in a focus group or a depth interview where they can speak freely, unfettered by questions needing answers. In these situations they have the time and space to explore for themselves what the brand means to them.

Qualitative research enables the researcher to spend time with the respondent. A focus group will usually last about two hours and an in-depth interview about an hour. Other qualitative methodologies such as ethnography or accompanied shopping will take half a day, so there is plenty of time to go beyond the 'top-of-mind' response and explore deeper motivations and associations.

Qualitative research allows us to explore perceptions and find out what is important to consumers. This methodology particularly suits situations when you don't really know what questions to ask. Rather than taking the expensive option of using a largely open-ended questionnaire where interviewers write down verbatim what respondents say, we do qualitative research first, to find out how consumers talk about the product or the market. Discovering in this way what factors or attributes are relevant enables us to design a follow-up quantitative survey to put numbers to the attitudes.

It is not always necessary to quantify qualitative research if the end itself is the understanding. Unfortunately, this is not always appreciated, and clients have been known to go ahead with major expenditure based on the results from eight people in a focus group. Be warned!

In-depth (depth) interviews

Individual depth interviews can be conducted face to face, over the phone or via Skype. They are usually one to one, with a semi-structured or unstructured approach, enabling a list of topics to be covered but not necessarily in a predetermined order. They are usually conducted by qualified qualitative researchers with skills in this area of exploratory research.

Depth interviews may use a list of open-ended questions that can be delivered in any order as just guidelines for the discussion. Interviewers may even be specialists in medical, financial or business matters, familiar with the specific terminology.

In-depth interviews tend to last between one and two hours. They are recorded, so that they can be analysed and transcribed later. This makes it easier for the interviewer to focus completely on the respondent, noticing body language and facial expressions and allowing the conversation to flow at the speed chosen by the respondent rather than dictated by how fast he or she can write. The interview may take place in:

- a central location such as a hotel or viewing studio
- the respondent's office
- the respondent's home.

The interviewer uses probing questions to delve below the surface response and get to subconscious motivations. In a depth interview the interviewer can allow the respondent to decide how much time they want to spend talking about each aspect of the subject, depending on how important that aspect is to them. This is quite different from a quantitative questionnaire, where the questionnaire designer determines the question order and the respondent cannot talk about anything else, nor answer more extensively than is required by the answer format.

How to run a depth interview

- **Dress to match the target:** wear a business suit for interviewing business respondents and older people; dress more casually for everyone else.
- **Open the interview using rapport** to show the respondent that you are genuinely interested in what they have to say. You can do this by matching their body language, how they are sitting, their tone of voice, volume and sentence length.
- **Assure them that there are no right or wrong answers,** and that anything they say will be of interest.

- **Tell them that their true opinions, attitudes and behaviour are what you want,** rather than what they might think they should do or what they think you would be impressed by.
- **Start with open questions** about the subject area, allowing them to tell you what's important and relevant to them.
- **Probe** to really understand what they mean; there should be no assumptions.
- **Use 'clean questions'** – these simply reflect back or repeat what they have said, e.g:
  - 'How do you do that?'
  - 'You say the packaging is boring?' (with an upward inflection)
  - 'In what way?'
- **Use indirect questioning,** e.g. 'Some might say...' or ' How do you think...would feel about that?'
- **Use personalization,** e.g. 'If the brand was a person, what sort of person would it be?' You can use pictures from magazines and newspapers to stimulate response or ask them which TV personality it would be, and why.
- **Keep the flow going** with changes of pace and time to reflect, do exercises, look at stimuli and ask a few closed questions, e.g. 'Do you like this one?'
- **Listen for the words they use** and use them yourself, even if they aren't words you'd normally use, because these show you are in rapport and on the same wavelength.
- **Use provocative questions** to move an interview forward, e.g. 'So you think all these packs are basically rubbish?' or, if they are fixated on one aspect that you feel you have covered enough, 'Right, so I know how you feel about that issue. Shall we park that and move on?' Humour, a smile and a slight tilt of the head show you are still in rapport and genuinely want to find out more.
- **Use role play** if appropriate, e.g. asking the respondent to 'sell' you the product you're talking about or asking them to imagine they are using the product.
- **Do a brand mapping exercise.** This is where you ask the respondent to sort a number of competitive brands into groups of similar and different ones, or arrange them in order of what they think are most expensive or more effective, or whatever criteria they have said was important, down to the least at the other end.

- **Use thematic apperception tests (bubble cartoons)** as a useful way of projecting one's feelings on to others. Draw a picture of a person using a particular brand or doing something relevant to the discussion, e.g. for a bank project draw someone going into a competitor bank and someone standing watching them, with a cartoon bubble. The respondent has to write in what that person is thinking. In doing so they are projecting their own thoughts.
- **Keep your own opinions to yourself.** They are not relevant but, if asked directly, suggest you tell them at the end of the interview because it is *their* opinions you want.

When depth interviews are preferable to focus groups

Sensitive subjects – e.g. sexual behaviour, debt, personal hygiene, serious illness and bereavement.

Confidentiality – e.g. where senior business people would not want to share business practice or company policy.

Key clients – e.g. in an 80:20 situation where a key client makes up most of the business, it would be respectful to interview them in person on their own and would increase the bond with the client company.

Individual information needed – if you need to understand an individual's behaviour and attitudes for the decision-making process, e.g. a buyer or specific business function.

Logistics – sometimes it can be difficult to get a group together because of consumers' location or work demands.

Segment building – to build a picture of the segment or market, the researcher can use the input from one interview as stimuli for the next, e.g. 'In the last interview I was told that...Is this something you experience?'

47

Mini-depths in a hall test environment

Mini-depths are interviews about 30 minutes long, often used in a hall test environment in addition to quantitative interviews. In this situation, a small number of respondents are specifically invited to take part in a depth interview in a separate room. They may be shown the same stimuli as the quantitative sample but the focus may be different.

> **Hall test** – a type of market research used for testing a product or advertisement, in which the researchers invite a group of consumers into a room and ask them their opinions of the product/advertisement.

This type of interview allows you to obtain a deeper understanding of the quantitative data. The interviewer may focus on less popular concepts in order to understand where a brand is performing poorly or on a specific aspect of the stimuli such as colour or font. A hall test can explore a specific target, such as respondents just below and above the sample age, to explore their reactions in more depth. This may help explain how a product or brand becomes aspirational or how people grow away from a brand. They can be used with rejecters of the brand or product, where the sample recruited is the core target market, to understand how people come to reject it, what they feel in depth and how they view competitive brands.

Paired depths and triads

Sometimes it can be beneficial to interview people in groups of two or three. Talking to a married couple, business partners, a mother and child or teenagers is particularly effective when researching decisions not taken individually, such as buying a car, a holiday, white goods or financial products. The interviewer can observe how decisions are made, who influences whom and what concerns each member of the pair or group.

Accompanied shopping

This methodology is used to understand the shopping process. The interviewer accompanies the respondent when shopping, having first asked the shopper whether they have a list or an idea about what to buy, either by brand or product type. They then go into the shop together and the interviewer combines observation skills with questioning about the purchasing decisions. The topics tend to be around choice between brands and the influence of the displays, promotion, prices and pack designs.

These interviews tend to be quite long, especially if they are preceded by an in-home interview, when the interviewer discusses what the shopper plans to buy in advance, looks through their cupboards and discusses brand perceptions in order to compare them with the in-store experience. These interviews may also be followed by a post-shopping interview to compare perceptions before and after. These extended accompanied shopping interviews can be extremely useful when researching a shop with people who don't usually shop there or non-buyers of a specific brand.

Any concerns that an interviewer accompanying a respondent will affect their behaviour can be overcome to some extent by conducting interviews in-store with shoppers already there. Questioning them about their behaviour is a much cheaper option but has to be done with retail consent, of course. It results in much shorter interviews because shoppers can usually spare only a short time, maybe minutes, but a number of mini-interviews can be conducted and recorded. Over the course of a day a picture can build up of the decision-making process.

Online depth interviews

An online qualitative version of the traditional in-depth interview can be conducted from the convenience of respondents' homes or offices. This is relevant nowadays, when 83 per cent of 18–54-year-olds use social media online. No special software is required to participate; respondents simply enter with one click from an email.

Service providers usually offer:

- chat-based or full webcam A/V discussions, designed for in-depth one-on-one qualitative interviewing
- automatic recording of the interview – video and audio
- tools to present stimulus, and allow respondents to point and annotate – respondents can also work on what you show them
- support for all Mac, Windows and Linux operating systems – Internet Explorer, Safari, Firefox, Opera and Google Chrome.

This methodology is ideal for most kinds of qualitative research projects because it offers:

- unique benefits over traditional methodologies – easier and cost-effective to engage respondents over as short or as long a time as you need, or to ensure anonymity of respondents if required
- a way to reach hard-to-find respondents, time-poor professionals, B2B participants and healthcare sector workers and patients

- a single, easy-to-use, integrated platform for new product development research, brand communications strategy research, ad testing, video concept testing, co-creation, usability testing and much more
- many benefits for international research projects (speed, live translation, research across multiple regions/time zones).

Focus groups

This is the methodology probably most frequently associated with qualitative market research. Focus groups are often used as the first part of a research project, to:

- whittle down a number of concepts to a smaller number before progressing to a quantitative stage
- explore brand imagery and perceptions within a competitive framework
- explore advertising or packaging communication
- understand the target market at a deeper level than quantitative research allows.

Typically, a project will comprise about six focus groups. They are usually done in pairs, to allow comparison such as users and non-users, regular and occasional users, older and younger, men and women, north and south. If the research is to take place in several countries, four groups might be set up in each country, selecting a location in each that is typical of the country (not always easy). Held in viewing studios, these can then be beamed across the Internet for clients worldwide to watch and comment on.

As with market segments, it is important that the respondents in each group be similar to one another and different in some significant way (to enable comparisons to be made) from the other groups. Although the groups are not meant to be representative in a quantifiable sense, the group should still represent the feelings and views of that type of respondent so that extrapolations can be made.

When focus groups are preferable to depth interviews

More detailed response

Group members or respondents interact, agreeing or disagreeing with comments made by others. The ensuing discussion tends to reveal much more about the nature of the response than people being interviewed singly.

More personal response

In groups where the members have something in common, such as having the same age children, working in the same type of industry or sharing a problem such as poor skin or hair, this creates a supportive environment. It often makes people feel more comfortable about revealing their innermost feelings compared to a one-on-one with an interviewer who does not share common ground.

TIP *A downside of focus groups is that, without skilled moderation, a dominant respondent can take over, intimidate other members and limit the insight achievable from the group.*

Group discussions or focus groups usually comprise six to eight respondents and take place in a viewing studio, the recruiter's home (more prevalent in the UK than the rest of Europe) and last about an hour-and-a-half to two hours. Extended group discussions can be up to three hours long and include tasks and more involved projective techniques such as role play.

Reconvened focus groups happen if a task is given during the first discussion, such as using a product for a week or two. The group then reconvenes to discuss what they have experienced. The task may be accompanied by a diary or questionnaire that respondents complete during the interim period and then bring to the reconvened discussion.

How to run a focus group

1 **Use a recruitment questionnaire or 'screener'** to ensure that respondents meet the sample requirement in terms of product usage, age, life stage or whatever has been agreed at the proposal stage. This needs to be done in advance of convening the group and again at the beginning of the discussion, because it can be disruptive to have someone in the group who should not be there.

2 **Choose an appropriate venue,** suitable for the target market. It should be somewhere people will feel relaxed, and not too far from where they live or work. Comfortable chairs and drinks and snacks should be provided, particularly for lengthy sessions or when the group takes place over lunch or during the evening.

3 **At the start of the discussion,** tell respondents:

- that they are being watched (if they are) and videoed, and that the video will not be shown on TV or to anyone not involved in the research (this is part of the MRS Code of Conduct)
- that they will not be identified by name or anything that might identify them, such as their role within a company or their face if it will be recognized
- the location of toilets and fire exits
- that there are no right or wrong answers, and that whatever they have to say has value
- that it is OK to disagree with other points of view and that, indeed, this can yield a more interesting discussion
- who else is in the room but not part of the group, such as a client or assistant
- that the moderator does not work for the client conducting the research and does not therefore know all the answers but is in effect sharing responsibility for answering the brief
- the nature of the task – a general idea of what you are going to be talking about
- who everyone is – briefly introduce the moderator and the respondents.

Make sure that everyone gets a chance to speak at an early stage; if they don't, they may clam up. Do this by asking everyone to introduce themselves in turn, or to introduce each other in pairs. Extend the process by asking them to describe something about themselves, such as their current favourite TV commercial.

4 Start with an open, general question about the topic, e.g. 'When I say...what immediately comes to mind?' This will make them get into the topic and forget about what they were doing before. You might want to note these top-of-mind associations on a pad or a flip chart and notice any patterns. This is often a good starting point, but make sure you have covered them all by the end of the discussion. If you miss out a particular word, the person who mentioned it will feel ignored; it might have been relevant for others too.

5 Now go through the topic guide, staying flexible and ready to tackle topics as they come up rather than in the order prescribed by the guide.

6 Check whether the client has any specific questions. You could say, 'My client has been fascinated by the discussion and wants me to thank you all for taking part. He just has a couple of questions he wanted to ask if that's OK.'

7 Sum up what you have learned as the moderator and start to bring the session to an end by collecting your papers together and so on. Then ask, 'Is there anything you want to add now that we've finished?' Something interesting may emerge then, such as a comment like, 'I'm surprised you didn't ask us about the...' or, 'I've just thought of another use for...'

The role of the moderator

The moderator has a vital role to play in every focus group. They have to create instant rapport in the group and fulfil an often complicated brief, obtaining everyone's views on a number of aspects of a topic, all within a limited time. Clients are inclined to overestimate what can be covered in an hour, which is often all that is available once initial introductions and final closings have been allowed for. They have to ensure that even the quieter respondents have their say and notice when someone's body language, if not their voice, suggests that they disagree with what someone has said.

Men in discussions tend to talk sequentially, that is one after another, but not necessarily responding to what another person has said. This can make it hard for the moderator to ensure that topics are actually discussed as opposed to simply being separate responses to a question raised. Women often talk simultaneously or back and forth, and by some miracle do respond to each other! This, however, makes it hard for the moderator to pick out individual contributions and follow up on them before the discussion moves to another phase. It also makes it hard for the transcriber of the recording to hear everything clearly and write it down for the analysis stage.

 In focus groups, use the same projective techniques as those described in the section above on depth interviews, but allow longer for each person to respond.

Online focus groups

Cheaper than running real-world focus groups, online focus groups – like online depth interviews – can be hugely beneficial for international projects and for business respondents. Recruited via email or online special interest groups, respondents can read other respondents' comments in response to the moderator's question and respond accordingly. However, there is an absence of rapport and no ability to read body language. They can use emoticons (smiley faces) but this is a poor substitute for having an experienced moderator with them who can absorb the different feelings in a group as he/she scans the participants constantly, sensing what is going on.

Ethnography

There are occasions when marketing needs a much more in-depth and detailed understanding of the consumer's life than can be obtained through conducting a depth interview or focus group. They want to see how consumers live, and spend time 'in their shoes' experiencing life as they do. Ethnography thus goes beyond mere reporting and attempts to interpret and give meaning to the experiences of different groups.

Summary

Today you learned that qualitative research is used to gather insight about the consumer or the market, how a brand is perceived, how a market is mapped, and how consumers respond to advertising, promotional or packaging concepts and new product ideas. The main methodologies are depth interviews and focus groups. The skills and techniques used by the depth interviewer and moderator are very similar. These skills involve getting and maintaining rapport, skilful use of indirect questions and projective techniques and the ability to respond with elegance and flexibility to ensure that the research brief is covered, but in a way that enables the group to feel free to contribute in a seemingly unstructured way.

The global market and advances in technology, as well as the widespread use of social media, mean that qualitative research is often conducted online. Although this is a bonus for many clients, it cannot replicate the experience of physically being in the same room that you get with the traditional focus group. Held in viewing studios, these can still be beamed across the Internet for clients worldwide to watch and comment on.

Fact-check (answers at the back)

1. When do you use qualitative research?
   a) When you can't afford quantitative ☐
   b) When you want to meet your consumers face to face ☐
   c) When you want insight rather than statistics ☐
   d) As the first stage in a quantitative project ☐

2. Which are the two main methodologies of qualitative research?
   a) Focus groups and ethnography ☐
   b) Depth interviews and hall tests ☐
   c) Accompanied shopping and focus groups ☐
   d) Focus groups and depth interviews ☐

3. What is rapport?
   a) The way the moderator or depth interviewer connects with the consumer ☐
   b) The way you analyse qualitative data ☐
   c) A projective technique ☐
   d) Online research ☐

4. What is a clean question?
   a) Not using swear words ☐
   b) Reflecting back what the respondent has just said as a question ☐
   c) Asking the same question twice ☐
   d) Asking the question indirectly ☐

5. When would you use charity vouchers as an incentive?
   a) If your client runs a charity ☐
   b) If you support a charity ☐
   c) If the respondent earns so much that the incentive would be very high ☐
   d) When you think the respondent would be more motivated by this gesture than the money ☐

6. When would you consider paired depths as a qualitative methodology?
   a) When the buying decision is joint ☐
   b) For financial research ☐
   c) When couples can't agree who should be interviewed ☐
   d) When you want to boost the sample size ☐

7. Why do we use a screener?
   a) To hide the respondent ☐
   b) To ensure you have the right respondents attending the research ☐
   c) To quantify background information about the respondent ☐
   d) To collect their names and addresses ☐

8. Where are focus groups usually held?
   a) In a hall ☐
   b) In a hotel ☐
   c) In a viewing studio ☐
   d) Online ☐

9. Do you have to tell respondents that they are being watched and recorded?
a) No, they would only get nervous ☐
b) Yes, because they may want to wear something nice ☐
c) No, they don't need to know ☐
d) Yes, it is part of the MRS Code of Conduct ☐

10. How would you start a depth interview or focus group?
a) Ask them their name ☐
b) Give them an open question ☐
c) Give them a cup of tea ☐
d) Ask them whether they use the brand ☐

WEDNESDAY

Quantitative market research

Yesterday we learned that qualitative research comprises depth interviews and focus groups that give us insight using indirect questioning techniques that – skilfully administered by an experienced moderator or interviewer – will elicit deep motivations and help us understand how consumers connect with our brand. This insight is particularly valuable at the start of a research project, when we want an initial understanding, terminology, an early response to creative material or concepts and to reduce the options in advance of a forthcoming quantitative survey.

You will probably have come across interviewers with clipboards who have approached you in the street and wanted to ask you questions. They will be doing quantitative market research. It differs from qualitative in the following ways.

- It provides conclusive information.
- It uses inflexible structured questioning.
- It gives limited opportunity to ask why or for explanations.
- It involves large samples (cells), which represent a defined universe.
- It uses a questionnaire.
- Analysis is by computer.
- Interpretation is objective.

Today you will learn when and how to use quantitative research.

When to use quantitative research

We learned on Sunday that market research provides information on which to base marketing decisions. When we need to be confident that the information can predict consumer reaction reliably, we conduct quantitative research because the sample we take will represent the universe of consumers in a statistically valid and replicable way.

We would not, for example, use focus groups to predict the percentage of 15–24-year-olds who would buy a new flavour of milkshake in a fast-food restaurant. Focus groups would be able to pare down the number of flavours, reduce a list of possible names for the flavour and react to designs for the pack or the point-of-sale material, but it would be too risky to rely for a purchasing decision on maybe six focus groups of eight respondents, a total of 48. This would be particularly true because this age group would comprise too many segments to be useful: boys and girls, schoolchildren, students, working people and different ethnic groups, incomes, tastes and usage of fast-food restaurants.

Using CAPI

> **CAPI (Computer-assisted personal interview)** – an interviewing or surveying technique that uses a computer-based questionnaire.

Nowadays, instead of using paper questionnaires, we can input data straight into a laptop and process it as soon as it is complete, rather than waiting for respondents to post their questionnaires back to the office. This system of data capture, called CAPI, also negates the need for manual data entry – taking the paper-based responses and 'punching' them into a computer program.

The other advantage of the CAPI system is that, instead of the interviewer having to follow instructions on the questionnaire itself, the computer program will take them to the next question automatically, based on the respondent's answer to the previous one. Any visuals, show cards, video clips of TV commercials or product demonstrations can also be presented to respondents. Where it would not be feasible to carry a laptop, a PenPad or similar can be used.

Face to face versus self-completion

Two types of questionnaire are used in quantitative surveys: face to face (interviewer administered) and self-completion. Tomorrow you will learn how to write both these types of questionnaire. Interviewers generally conduct their quota of interviews face to face, using either a paper questionnaire or a laptop where they input the answers, which are then uploaded straight into the analysis software in the office. These are done in the street, in homes and in offices. They are also the main type of questionnaire used in hall tests.

When the interview is done using personal interviewing methods, where there is direct contact between the interviewer and respondent regardless of how the data is inputted, the data is robust for the following reasons.

- The interviewer is trained to administer the questionnaire, ensure it is complete, delivered as per instructions and delivered to the respondent specified by the quota.
- Any complex questions can be repeated and explained – but not interpreted, as this would introduce the interviewer's own interpretation and influence the answer given.
- Open-ended questions can be included to elicit 'likes' and 'dislikes' and 'other answers'.
- They allow the interviewer the opportunity to probe ambiguous answers given to open-ended questions so that a full answer is given that can be coded for analysis.
- Stimuli can be shown to the respondent at a specific point in the interview rather than when the respondent opens the envelope or the email.

The robustness of face-to-face, interviewer-administered questionnaires comes at a cost: interviewer training and quality control are expensive and fewer interviews can be done in a day than using online survey methods. Another argument sometimes made is that interviewers might only approach people who look friendly and with whom they feel comfortable. They might avoid houses with dogs or noisy children, poor and run-down areas and people who look busy, and the result will be a skewed sample.

Self-completion questionnaires may be sent by post, by email – possibly with an email link to a website – or by text. Very simple ones are often displayed on till displays at shops and petrol stations. Our local one asks, 'Did you have to queue today?' or, 'Was the person serving you polite?' or, 'Did the shop look tidy?' The respondent can choose whether to complete the questionnaire, whether to answer all the questions and how to interpret the questions. If they get bored halfway through, there is no one to encourage them to complete it and, if they want to, they could answer incorrectly or pass it to someone else to complete. The fact that self-completion questionnaires cannot be controlled is their main and serious disadvantage, but targeting them to respondents who have a vested interest in responding with integrity reduces the chances of them being 'spoiled'.

Locations for interviews

Quantitative interviewing takes place in a range of environments, which vary in their ease of interviewing. More and more quantitative interviewing now takes place online, but plenty of surveys still take place in the home, on the street, in the workplace and in halls.

In the home

In-home interviews

In the past, face-to-face interviewing was done on the doorstep or in the home with mothers, about domestic matters such as grocery shopping. Today fewer people are at home during the day, and home security allows residents to preview callers before opening the door. Interviewers are understandably reluctant to work in the evenings when there would be more chance of catching someone at home. Therefore, when a survey requires this type of interview, it has to be pre-booked and often takes place in a central venue such as a hall or hotel.

Product placement

In some cases you may want to test a new product in the home over a period of time to find out how consumers' usage of the product changes as they become more familiar with it. Products that need home preparation or construction, such as a flat pack or a decorating or DIY product, lend themselves well to product placement.

Consumers are recruited using a basic quantitative questionnaire about their usage and behaviour, home situation, family composition and then chosen to take part in the product placement test according to the criteria set by the research brief. The product will be placed and an interview conducted to establish consumers' expectations and initial response to the product. During the placement they will keep a diary recording their experience during usage. The product will then be collected and another interview carried out to cover their experience overall and their response to pricing, key features, benefits and the perceived target market.

On the street

Street interviews, which are much cheaper than in-home interviews, may take place in shopping malls (where permission can be obtained) or on the street. Street interviewing may be adversely affected by the weather and the busyness of the available subjects, so it is important that the questionnaire length be manageable, usually 15–20 minutes maximum.

Interviewers generally try to find a good location where they will have access to the target sample, such as outside a school for parents. This is obviously more difficult if the target sample is normally very busy or working in offices. Since most shoppers try to avoid anyone bearing a clipboard, they may not necessarily represent the sample if they are amenable. Also there can be distractions on the street with children losing patience, dogs, traffic noise and simply managing the questionnaire, show cards and maybe other stimuli.

Intercept and exit interviews

Retailers and owners of theme parks, airports or other venue-based business may conduct intercept or exit interviews with customers as they interact with the attraction or as they leave. Clearly there would not be permission issues in this situation and customers' opinions can be captured at the time they experienced the service, which makes the data very valuable. Questions usually relate to respondents' attitudes to quality of service, customer satisfaction, signage, cleanliness and range of facilities. Respondents can be 'paid' with a money-off voucher for the attraction on a future visit and interviewers can achieve a good 'hit rate' as everyone will probably qualify.

Shops and supermarkets

Mystery shopping

This involves interviewers going incognito into shops or supermarkets, hotels or other service delivery points to report back on what they find. They fill in a questionnaire after their visit and usually have tasks to complete, such as asking staff where something is, checking toilets or phoning them to check how they deal with enquiries. Staff are made aware that they will receive visits from mystery shoppers but not when.

Store checks

Interviewers check the shelves of supermarkets for a particular manufacturer. They record what products are there, how many shelf facings there are, the selling price, whether any promotions are being offered and how much stock is held.

In the workplace

Face-to-face interviewing in a business environment is done for products and services used in the workplace. This can be an expensive option compared to online questionnaires because it often requires interviewers to have specialized knowledge and contacts to get past the receptionist or PA (who tends to block such calls from market researchers) in order to identify the correct person to interview. Incentives usually have to be offered and permission given from the PR department.

Pharmaceutical and medical companies use face-to-face interviewing, and interviewers are often former doctors and nurses who have the contacts and knowledge of the market and the terminology. Incentives are usually paid for taking part. Interviewers will use the café or public areas of hospitals for doing the interviews, with the permission of the hospital or clinic.

Hall tests and mall intercepts

These are popular methods of interviewing because interviewers can work inside once they have recruited someone from the street according to the quota set. In this indoor environment it is easy to set up mock shops, laptops showing TV ads, products to view or test, concept boards and anything that would be difficult for the interviewer to carry around.

In the UK, halls are usually part of a community building, pub, hotel or leisure centre or attached to a church. The room is hired for the day and tables and chairs set up for the interviewers. A supervisor will control the sample and manage the fieldwork.

In the US these indoor interviews are called 'mall intercepts', where there is a room near the entrance to the shopping mall and respondents are taken in there in much the same way as a hall test. In many cases market research companies have their office in a shopping mall and use one of their own rooms.

Although the cost of hall hire may have to be factored into the budget, the quality of the interviews and length of questionnaire that can be administered in this more comfortable environment make it a good choice for surveys that cannot for practical reasons be conducted on the street. The other advantage of a hall test or mall intercept is that clients can attend and listen to the interviews and get a better understanding of their consumer.

The main disadvantage with hall tests and mall intercepts is that they are only suitable for a sample that is likely to be on the street near the hall or other venue at the time. Supervisors tend to know which halls will suit the sample from past experience and will often need to pre-recruit respondents who will not naturally be there.

Car clinics, mobile phone clinics and computer clinics are all a form of hall test. The format is identical but the event takes place in a car showroom or other large room or hall where pre-recruited customers are invited to appraise new models.

Panels

Many large companies and research agencies set up panels of consumers or customers, to whom they regularly send a questionnaire or a diary to complete about their buying behaviour and use of specific products and services. Panels tend to be ongoing so that information can be tracked and changes observed in response to price changes, distribution, special offers, promotions, advertising and new competitors entering the market.

Maintaining a panel is time-consuming and costly. The make-up of the panel needs to be constantly checked to ensure that its profile represents the market. As members leave, new ones need to be recruited to take their place.

Response rates for panels are high because members making a commitment to complete regular questionnaires are often 'paid' in vouchers and free gifts. However, this can skew results because the fact that they have agreed to take part may be because they have a strong opinion on the product category, have a lot of spare time or are different in some other way from those who would never take part in such a panel.

Panel data used to be collected via paper questionnaires and paper diaries but this has now largely been replaced with electronic data capture.

Selling questionnaire space

Companies and agencies running a panel for their product may sell space on the questionnaire to other companies in the same market with the same consumer profile but in non-competing product categories. This is a cost-effective approach.

bus surveys

e surveys offering a large sample, often on a
asis and targeting specific types of consumers,
such as families or motorists. Clients can buy space on the
questionnaire and just pay for their own questions and the
analysis and reporting of them. This keeps costs to a minimum
as they are charged according to the number of questions
placed. Careful management of the survey avoids questions
from competing companies in the same product category and
ensures that questions are placed in an order that will make
the questionnaire flow well for the respondents. You can find
a list of research agencies offering omnibus surveys in the
ESOMAR directory, available online.

Omnibus surveys are carried out face to face or via the
telephone or Internet and take place at regular intervals such
as weekly or monthly. This means that companies who want
to track brand awareness before and after an advertising
campaign can obtain valuable data based on large sample
sizes that would be too expensive to consider any other way.

Summa

Today you learned that quantitative resea offers a range of ways of measuring consumer behaviour, usage of and attitudes towards products and services, awareness of brand and advertising, price sensitivity, customer satisfaction and purchasing intentions.

Companies can conduct their own survey or buy into panels and omnibus surveys, which for small companies and products in niche markets can be a cost-effective option. Survey methodology will depend on a number of factors such as the size and portability of the product, percentage who have heard of it or use it, the accessibility of the sample to be surveyed and the budget.

Today you were able to compare the methodology of qualitative research with the more structured approach of quantitative research. Many surveys combine the two because they offer complementary insight: the deeper motivational issues of qualitative tell you the *how* and the *why*, while the quantitative tells you *what* consumers do *when* and *where*.

Tomorrow we will learn how to ask different types of question in order to get answers that will be actionable and meet the marketing objectives.

MONDAY

TUESDAY

WEDNESDAY

THURSDAY

FRIDAY

SATURDAY

act-check (answers at the back)

1. If you wanted to test a large product designed for the home, what methodology would you choose?
a) Hall test ❏
b) Telephone interviews ❏
c) Street interviews ❏
d) Product placement ❏

2. If you want to research a brand in its infancy and track brand share, how would you do it?
a) Omnibus survey ❏
b) Panel ❏
c) CAPI ❏
d) Diary ❏

3. Usage and attitude surveys are examples of what type of market research?
a) Qualitative ❏
b) Quantitative ❏
c) Panels ❏
d) Hall tests ❏

4. What is CAPI?
a) Consumer application of paper industry ❏
b) Cleverly applied paper interview ❏
c) Computer-assisted personal interview ❏
d) Consumer-assisted paper interview ❏

5. What is an intercept interview?
a) Where you stop a consumer and interview them where they are ❏
b) Where you stop a consumer and place a product with them ❏
c) Where you stop a consumer and book a depth interview with them ❏
d) Where you stop a consumer and invite them to a hall test ❏

6. How do you pay for an omnibus survey?
a) You pay for the whole questionnaire ❏
b) You pay for the whole questionnaire minus the agency's questions ❏
c) You only pay for the background demographics ❏
d) You just pay for your own questions ❏

7. Which of the following statements is true?
a) Self-completion questionnaires cannot be used in the US ❏
b) It is hard to control the quality of response in self-completion questionnaires ❏
c) People don't like filling in questionnaires ❏
d) You always get a poor response rate with self-completion questionnaires ❏

8. Which of the following is not a form of quantitative data capture?
a) Diary ☐
b) Video ☐
c) Paper questionnaire ☐
d) Online poll ☐

9. Which of the following is an example of skew?
a) Interviewers selecting people they like the look of to interview ☐
b) Respondents choosing to be interviewed in a hall ☐
c) Respondents signing up to paid survey sites online ☐
d) All of the above ☐

10. Why does interviewing take place in the home less than it used to?
a) People don't like to answer the door to strangers and invite them in ☐
b) Interviewers don't like to work at night ☐
c) Interviewers prefer hall tests ☐
d) Clients can't afford them ☐

THURSDAY

Questionnaire and topic guide design

The questionnaire is the data collection tool used primarily in quantitative research. Its equivalent in qualitative research is the topic guide, which the moderator of the focus group or depth interview uses to lead respondents through a series of issues they need to cover in depth. You will learn how to write a topic guide today as well.

It is a common misconception that writing a questionnaire or topic guide is simply a matter of writing down the questions to which you want answers. In fact, questionnaire design is a skilled job. Questions need to be:

- clear and unambiguous so that everyone will interpret them the same way
- impartial, and not lead respondents to answer in a particular way
- free of assumptions, e.g. 'When you recycle, do you...'
- short and easy to follow
- asked one at a time
- clear and easy to understand
- free of jargon.

Understanding the principles of questionnaire design will guarantee that the answers you need will indeed result from the questions.

Basic principles of questionnaire design

Whatever research project you undertake, a questionnaire or focus group guide will need to be written and agreed internally and with the research supplier. A quantitative questionnaire will comprise a number of typewritten pages on screen or paper and will be completed by the respondent (self-completion) or with the help of an interviewer. The respondent or interviewer records the responses on the page or computer by circling or clicking 'codes' or writing in answers that will be coded at the analysis stage, discussed tomorrow.

As each question is answered, an instruction, either written into the software or given to the interviewer, leads the respondent to the next question. Instructions are written on the questionnaire to inform the interviewer or the respondent whether they can give one answer (single code) or more than one answer (multi-code) and whether they need to probe or prompt. **Probing** is asking for more information and **prompting** is suggesting answers from a list of possible answers printed on the questionnaire.

We will start by explaining the different types of question you can use in the questionnaire and then explain the structure.

Public relations

Based on their experience of a market research interview, respondents will form a view of the brand and the company behind the survey. We want them to believe that the client is genuinely interested in what they have to say and will bear their views in mind as they develop their marketing strategy in future. We want to leave them happy to be respondents again, even if not for our survey.

Types of question

Open questions

Open, or open-ended, questions are those that allow a respondent to answer in their own words. The interviewer (or the respondent in a self-completion questionnaire) writes them down in full (known as **verbatim** in quantitative research) or records them (known as **quotes** in qualitative research), either online or offline. When designing your questionnaire, it is vital to allow plenty of space to write in the answers.

Examples of open-ended questions are:

- 'What are your first impressions of the new pack design?'
- 'What is the main message of this TV ad?'
- 'Who do you think this product would appeal to?'

Sometimes a question will be asked as an open-ended question but the interviewer will have some pre-codes (possible answers) to circle on the questionnaire, which will cover the likely answers but which do not preclude other answers. For example, in the question above about the main message of a TV ad, the agency will have specific words they want to check for, such as, 'Brand X gives you three of your five a day', 'Children will enjoy brand X' or 'Brand X is crunchy'. If the respondent mentions these, they can immediately be coded to save all the verbatims having to be analysed, which will save costs. In this example the research agency did not want to prompt respondents with the possible answers but leave them to mention them by using an open question.

Once the respondent has answered the open question, the interviewer probes for more information if her instructions say to do so. Instructions could be 'Probe fully', which means that the interviewer has to ask, 'What else?' or, 'In what way is the brand...?' She continues to probe until the respondent says, 'No, there's nothing else.' If the instructions say 'Probe to clarify', the interviewer has to probe enough to know and write down exactly what the respondent means. For example, if they say, 'I really like it' the interviewer would ask, 'What do you like about it?' because simply saying they like it does not give enough information.

In a focus group topic guide or a depth interview all the questions are open.

Closed questions

Closed questions come in three forms: dichotomous, multiple choice and scales.

Dichotomous questions

These offer a straight 'yes or no' option, e.g. 'Do you own a car?' or, 'Do you ever buy furniture polish?' or a simple choice of two answers, such as:

- *Do you own your car outright or do you have a finance arrangement?*

  – Own car outright ☐ – Finance agreement ☐

In some cases we might add an option for 'Don't know' for questions like, 'Does anyone in your household have a bank account?' because the respondent may not know if their partner has one.

Dichotomous questions are often used as filters.

- In an omnibus questionnaire, where a client has paid for a series of questions on a gardening product, he would only want to ask questions of people who have a garden. The filter questions would be dichotomous: 'Do you have a garden?' The answer would be yes or no. Anyone answering no would move straight on to the next set of questions from another client.

- It might be necessary to establish whether a respondent has any connection to the company or industry. For example, 'Do you or any of your close friends or family work or have they ever worked in any of these industries [reads out list]?' Yes/No
- They may be used to analyse why they prefer A to B after their answer to a question such as, 'Which of these two packs do you prefer, Pack A or Pack B?'

Multiple-choice questions

The majority of behavioural or usage questions used in market research questionnaires are multiple choice. They may ask how often a customer buys a particular product type or brand, where they buy it, how and when they serve it and so on. The questions give the respondent a number of options from which they are told how many they can choose. The options are usually to choose 'one' (single code) or 'all that apply' (multi-code). The simplest form of multiple-choice question relates to the respondent's age. For example:

- *Which of the following age groups are you in?*

  - 15–19   ❑   – 25–34   ❑
  - 20–24   ❑   – 35 or over   ❑

All the options are written on a card that is shown to the respondent, who chooses one or more answers as instructed. It is therefore important that each answer is different from the other, with no overlap between the questions. The question may allow more than one answer. For example:

- *Where do you a) <u>usually</u> buy petrol? or b) <u>sometimes</u> buy petrol?*

	Usually Single code	*Sometimes* Multi-code
– The nearest petrol station to my house	❑	❑
– The nearest petrol station to my work	❑	❑
– The one with the cheapest petrol	❑	❑
– The nearest one when I need to fill up	❑	❑
– One that sells a good range of groceries	❑	❑
– One that has a good loyalty card	❑	❑

Questions of this type often use quite complex grids. For example:

Where do you buy...most often?

	Local grocers	Shop online	Supermarket	Cash and Carry	Discount store	Off-licence
Wine	☐	☐	☐	☐	☐	☐
Beer	☐	☐	☐	☐	☐	☐
Soft drinks	☐	☐	☐	☐	☐	☐
Crisps/nuts	☐	☐	☐	☐	☐	☐
Mixers	☐	☐	☐	☐	☐	☐
Spirits	☐	☐	☐	☐	☐	☐

Although it is not printed on the card the respondent is shown, there will be a 'Don't know' or 'Not applicable' option printed on the questionnaire. There is often also an 'Other' option which may or may not be shown to the respondent. In most cases interviewers will have to write in any 'Other' answers given.

Routing is either printed on the questionnaire, for example 'Go to Q5', or programmed into the questionnaire on the computer. These instructions direct the interviewer to the next question according to the answer given to this one. If the client wants to know more about people who buy soft drinks from an off-licence/package store (if they answer that they do in the above question), the interviewer will next ask them more about this and not ask the question if they buy soft drinks elsewhere.

The multiple-choice answers for each question are often derived from qualitative research, but they may also correspond to industry classifications, categories used in continuous tracking surveys purchased or designed to tie in with other research so that comparisons can be made.

If your research is pan-European or international, the questionnaire will contain answers applicable to other markets. As the survey will be analysed and processed using the same computer program, it is crucial that each code on the questionnaire corresponds to only one possible answer across all the questionnaires, regardless of different translations of it used in other markets.

Scales

Several types of scale are used in questionnaire design to gather attitudinal information, such as customer satisfaction or perceptions of quality. Usually each point on the scale will be assigned a number. For example:

● *How would you rate the quality of the meal you have just eaten on a scale of 1–5, where 1 is very low quality and 5 is very high quality?*

> *1   2   3   4   5*

Another way of presenting the scale is using words, which are shown to respondents on a show card. For example:

● *How would you rate the quality of the meal you have just eaten using the words on this card?*

| Very low quality | Low quality | Neither low nor high quality | High quality | Very high quality |

Sometimes this type of scale is used to ask a comparative question, such as:

● *How would you describe the meal you have just eaten compared to what you expected, using the words on this card?*

Much worse than expected	*Slightly worse than expected*	*About the same as expected*	*Slightly better than expected*	*Much better than expected*

Using the satisfaction version, the question would look like this:

● *How satisfied are you with the meal you have just eaten?*

Very unsatisfied	*Quite unsatisfied*	*Neither unsatisfied nor satisfied*	*Quite satisfied*	*Very satisfied*

You will notice that all the examples so far have allowed the respondent to choose a middle position on the scale. However, sometimes the research objectives require the findings to be clearly positive or negative. For example, if the research is to decide on a new pack design for a well-established brand, it may be important to ask existing customers of the brand to rate each design along a scale like this:

Much worse than the current pack	*Slightly worse than the current pack*	*Slightly better than the current pack*	*Much better than the current pack*

Other scales used in questionnaires are lists of attributes of a product or brand which respondents are asked to reorder by how important they are to them. They will tell the interviewer which one is in first position, second, third, etc., and the interviewer will record the number on their questionnaire. At the analysis stage, all those attributes named as top priority will be given a score of, say, ten (if there are ten attributes), nine to the second most important, eight to the third and so on.

A variation on this is when a list of attributes or variables is given to the respondent and they have to allocate a number of points to each, out of a maximum of ten. The benefit of this type of question is that it separates more clearly than the previous technique those aspects that are most important and those that are almost irrelevant.

These scales have all been 'rating scales' and are used regularly to ascertain customer satisfaction or determine their response to various attributes of the product, pack, TV commercial, etc. We use what are known as **'Likert' scales** to collect attitudinal data. In this process, statements may be developed from qualitative research that reflects a diversity of attitudes about the product or service. These are listed on the questionnaire and on a show card given to the respondent. They are asked the extent to which they agree or disagree with each, like this:

● *I would like to read out a number of comments other people have made about this restaurant. Please could you use this card to answer how much you agree or disagree with each statement?*

	Disagree strongly	Disagree slightly	Neither agree nor disagree	Agree slightly	Agree strongly
The portion size is too small	1	2	3	4	5
The food is attractively presented	1	2	3	4	5
The waiting staff are courteous	1	2	3	4	5
Service is efficient	1	2	3	4	5
The menu offers a wide range	1	2	3	4	5
The decor is pleasing	1	2	3	4	5

The efficacy of this type of scale is dependent on:

- the choice of statements being based on what people have actually said
- a good mix of ones they will agree with and ones they will disagree with so they don't get bored answering the same every time
- clearly expressed opinions that respondents understand
- avoiding generalizations, such as 'The portion size is always too small'
- not leading the respondent with exaggerated statements such as 'The portion size is far too small'.

Structure of the questionnaire

The flow of a questionnaire or topic guide is very important. It should have an introduction and a clear beginning, middle and end, as this is most logical from the respondents' viewpoint.

The introduction

Either in a covering letter or on the questionnaire itself, it is essential to tell the respondent who is administering the questionnaire. You do not have to tell them the actual client and, indeed, this information would skew the results. They simply need to know what the product category is. They also need to know:

- that the interviewer is trained and complies with the Market Research Code of Conduct – at this point interviewers usually show their interviewer identity card which should have their photo and name on it
- that their answers are confidential and will be inputted anonymously
- that they will not be contacted afterwards except to check that the interview has taken place (back-check)
- how long the interview will take.

The screening questions

These types of question come at the beginning of the questionnaire and are designed as filters, to ensure that the only people answering your questions will be those you have selected as your target market. Normal exclusions are:

● people who work for your company or your competitors or who have family or friends who do, because they will have an untypical response to the questions and you may not want your competitors knowing about the survey
● people who work in market research, advertising or marketing who may have a more professional attitude to the questions and try to second-guess what they are about
● those who have answered a questionnaire on this product category in the previous six months
● those who would be unlikely to be aware of your product or service or who may not be in your target market
● people who haven't heard of your brand, haven't bought your brand or wouldn't consider buying your brand
● those who don't buy your product category, e.g. cat food
● people not resident in the UK
● students
● people out of work or with no main income as they may not be able to buy the product.

Be aware that the number of filters you apply will affect the 'hit rate' or the number of interviews an interviewer will achieve per day. As they are usually paid a day rate, you don't want to filter out more respondents than is necessary. On the other hand, you don't want to waste an interview on someone whose views you are not concerned with. Interviewers are trained to find the sample they are looking for, so direction to them about your target sample will be helpful.

'Questioning is the door of knowledge.'

Irish saying

The main sections

Respondents find it easier to follow a questionnaire if it has structure with clearly defined sections. Start each section with a brief explanation of what that section is about, for example: 'This section is about your purchasing of cat food.'

It is generally advisable to start with specific closed questions that are easy to answer, such as what they have bought and where, and how they use it and how often. These are usually presented as multiple-choice grids with the items down the left-hand side and columns for each option – such as frequency of purchase – so that they or the interviewer only need circle one code per product.

There should always be an option for 'Never' and 'Don't know'. This is because the computer analysis has to read a code in every column and cannot read additional comments by the respondent or interviewer. These additional comments have first to be coded and those codes inputted. Coding adds cost to the processing of the survey, so it is important to provide all the possible answers on the questionnaire at the design stage.

Next, add some scales to elicit attitudes, and finish with some open-ended questions that allow the respondent, now nicely warmed up, to express their views in their own words.

The classification and follow-up

Questionnaires usually end with the interviewer collecting demographic information about the respondent, which will be used to analyse their questionnaire. The usual data collected is:

- age within a range
- gender
- occupation of head of household
- address and contact telephone number.

At the end of the interview, the interviewer will thank the respondent and tell them that the only follow-up may be from their supervisor, who may call to check that the interview has been conducted according to the instructions given. Usually a 10 per cent back-check is conducted. This comprises checking that the interview really has taken place, where it took place and when. One or two questions will be selected to ask during the back-check call to ensure that the information was correctly recorded.

Feedback

At the end of the interviewing process each interviewer completes a report on how the survey went, so that research agencies can learn from their feedback and make amendments next time that survey is done. However, when a tracking or continuous survey is being done, this process rarely results in changes being made. This is because it is essential that question wording and order remain exactly the same so that only changes in the response are tracked.

Piloting your questionnaire

The importance of piloting a questionnaire cannot be overestimated. Piloting will ensure that the questions posed will result in the data necessary to inform the marketing decision that needs to be taken as a result of the survey.

Even those with many years' experience in a product category can find that some of their questions are not understood, ambiguous, in the wrong order or missing obvious pre-codes. The interviewers then have to write in an answer as 'Other' that should have been included in the multiple-choice list. This extra coding is expensive and valuable data can be missed.

The length of a questionnaire is also important, since it will determine how many an interviewer can achieve in a day. Very long questionnaires will get a high dropout rate, with respondents losing interest halfway through. Therefore most research agencies will allow time to pilot the questionnaire in each country where research is taking place. This also tests the accurate translation of the questionnaire.

During the pilot, a number of experienced interviewers will conduct interviews across the target sample. They then complete a pilot report, commenting on each question and how long it took, and whether it was understood. They will also note all 'Other' answers. The questionnaire is amended in the light of the interviewer reports before it is put out in 'the field' – in other words before the real interviewing starts.

Structure of the topic guide

The topic guide is used in a qualitative focus group. It lists topics and stimuli to be shown and does not look like a list of questions. It will be relatively unstructured, listing the topics to cover in whatever order works best for the group. The moderator running the group will be guided by where the interest is and what the respondents bring up spontaneously, because these issues will be most relevant and therefore most important to the product category or brand.

While a questionnaire uses a funnel approach, moving from quick and easy closed questions at the beginning to open questions at the end, in a focus group the design is more 'egg-timer' shaped. Here the first questions are open, to explore what is relevant and current, and they then become more searching and specific. The final questions are again more wide-ranging, to cover any topics as yet untapped.

For more on running a focus group, see Tuesday's chapter.

Summary

Whether you are doing qualitative or quantitative research, the emphasis should always be on eliciting the information you need in the way that will make sense to the respondent. We want the conversation to flow and build understanding and rapport, so that respondents feel positive about being interviewed and about the market research process.

For these reasons in quantitative research good questionnaire design is vital for the success of a project. Questions need to be carefully worded and the questionnaire must have a layout and structure that will enable users to find their way around it easily. Piloting is also a crucial element of questionnaire development, ensuring that the questions posed will result in the data needed.

In focus groups questioning is less structured but just as important, and the topic guide is an essential tool when the moderator is formulating questions in the light of what is said in the discussion.

Tomorrow we will learn how completed questionnaires and other data are analysed and used to inform marketing decisions.

Fact-check (answers at the back)

1. What is a closed question?
a) One with an obvious answer ❏
b) A question that is not misleading ❏
c) A question that has a number of possible answers ❏
d) A question that is not leading ❏

2. What is a Likert scale?
a) The chance for respondents to say to what extent they agree or disagree with a number of attitude statements ❏
b) A list of attributes that respondents place in order of priority ❏
c) A scale where the respondent scores each attribute ❏
d) Where the respondent says what they think in their own words ❏

3. What is a screening question?
a) A question about the respondent's demographics ❏
b) An introductory question ❏
c) A question at the end ❏
d) A question to check the respondent's eligibility to form part of the sample ❏

4. Which of these is an example of a leading question?
a) Don't you think dog food should taste of what it says on the can? ❏
b) When you buy dog food from a supermarket, how much do you pay? ❏
c) Which dog food brand do you buy most often? ❏
d) Do you ever buy dog food? ❏

5. Which of these is a dichotomous question?
a) How many times a week do you watch TV – once, twice or three times a week, etc.? ❏
b) Do you watch TV more than once a week? Yes/No ❏
c) How much do you watch TV advertising? ❏
d) What do you think about watching TV? ❏

6. Which of these is an open-ended question?
a) A question that is very long and difficult to understand ❏
b) A question with five possible answers ❏
c) A question you can't answer ❏
d) A question you can answer in your own words ❏

7. A well-designed questionnaire has to have what?
a) Clearly introduced sections ❏
b) A good introduction ❏
c) Clear layout ❏
d) All of the above ❏

8. What is the difference between a questionnaire and a topic guide?
a) A topic guide is a list of topics to be covered, not questions ❏
b) Questionnaires are filled in by a respondent ❏
c) A topic guide is agreed with the client ❏
d) You don't have to follow a topic guide ❏

9. What is routing?
a) Supporting the client ☐
b) Instructions that take the interviewer to the next question ☐
c) Instructions to the interviewer on how to ask the questions ☐
d) A list of multiple-choice answers ☐

10. What is a filter question used to ensure?
a) That only a sub-section of the sample answer some questions ☐
b) That only those eligible to answer the questions are asked them ☐
c) That no one in marketing answers the questions ☐
d) That the interviewer has done their job correctly ☐

FRIDAY

Research analysis

Today we will look at what happens to the data collected through questionnaires, focus groups and depth interviews.

Quantitative surveys often involve thousands of questionnaires, so they cannot be analysed by hand. Even smaller surveys of hundreds of questionnaires need computer analysis to be able to compare different sub-segments within the market, and probably different geographical markets too.

Qualitative data from focus groups and depth interviews analysed in a different way and, since the results are not statistically significant, they may later be verified with a quantitative survey. The focus in qualitative research is on gaining insight and understanding and the exploration of issues, not facts and figures.

Today you will learn about the different types of analysis you can ask for and what you should be checking, to ensure that your data is valid and can be relied on when making marketing decisions.

Analysis is the penultimate stage of a market research survey. The results still need to be interpreted and presented, and we will examine this final element of market research tomorrow.

Quantitative analysis

It is extremely unlikely that you will be personally responsible for the analysis of questionnaires because this is done by the technology. Before this can happen, completed questionnaires must first be checked against the quota the interviewers or supervisors were set. Each interviewer will have been given a number of interviews to achieve in each demographic or user type, such as users and non-users.

There are three main stages in the questionnaire analysis process:

1 coding
2 data entry
3 production of tables.

1 Coding

Coding is the process that assigns numerical codes to answers on the questionnaire that don't already have one. These include answers to open-ended questions and answers written in as 'Other answer' at the end of a pre-coded multiple-choice list. Sometimes, if interviewers have missed a question or coded two answers where only one was required, these have to be corrected by reading through the questionnaire and making an educated guess as to what the correct answer should be. If that can't be done, the respondent may be phoned to ask that question again.

Grouping responses

Coders take a sample of each interviewer's questionnaires so that they have about 100 to work on. From these, taking one question at a time, they list the verbatim responses written on the questionnaire. They then go through the list, grouping together similar responses, bearing in mind the research objectives to ensure that specifics that need to be kept separate – because they are of particular interest – are not grouped with other responses.

For example, if colour is relevant, it would be kept separate from comments about appearance or visual appeal that are more general. In this way, when the analysis is done and tables produced, the researcher can compare across the sample those for whom colour was an issue, either positively or negatively. Positive and negative comments would be listed separately in any case. Some answers will be easy to combine, such as words that mean much the same thing, for example 'good price', 'reasonable price' and so on. Another example might be positive comments on the 'text', 'copy', 'writing' or 'wording' where respondents have simply used different words to describe the same thing.

The coder working on the project usually checks the list of verbatims and suggests which could be grouped together. The coder then suggests other groupings that would combine answers that are more diverse, such as 'other negative comments' and 'other positive comments'. At this stage it is important to keep in mind the research objectives and in particular the specific aspects or attributes of the survey.

The code frame

If the research is being conducted across several countries, the 'lead country' will provide the code frame (list of codes) that all the other countries will use. This can sometimes present problems where words in one country have a slightly different meaning or words that are positive in one country are negative in another. The lead coder will usually send the proposed code frame to the colleagues in other markets to check that it will work for their market as well.

Numerical codes are allocated to the most frequently occurring responses (usually about 10–15). Once the pre-codes are agreed, they are given to the coding department and coding proper will take place. By the end of this stage all the questionnaires have codes marked on them, usually in red biro and circled, as well as the pre-codes already circled or marked on the questionnaire by the interviewer.

Keyword coding

Some coders will use 'keyword coding', which speeds up the process a great deal. They simply code specific words that are mentioned and which the researcher has asked them to record specifically. The downside of this is where a respondent will use a whole phrase to describe their feeling, which might be better described by a word they haven't used. Nevertheless, it is reduced to keywords.

For example, a respondent might have said, 'I really liked the overall design, it looks classy and stylish, as if it is a more expensive product than it really is.' Keyword coding would result in codes allocated for 'classy', 'stylish' and 'expensive', but the overall comment might suggest the design is aspirational. In this context 'expensive' is a positive, but if combined with negative comments – that the product looks, say, 'too expensive' or 'is expensive' – it will produce a skewed response.

2 Data entry

While computer-assisted interviews and web-based surveys are automatically uploaded into a computer, paper-based questionnaires have to be manually uploaded. An operator has to enter all the codes of the questionnaires being scanned in.

The data is then cleaned of inconsistencies, such as:

- missing codes
- multi-codes where only one was allowed
- problems not picked up by the coders.

Problems might include respondents answering questions they did not need to answer because the routing was not followed correctly.

3 Production of tables

While the coding and data entry are taking place, the researcher decides how to present the data. They may look at the 'hole count', which is a read-out from the computer program telling them how many responses there are for each code. This is an early 'top-line' feel of the data that will give them an idea of what the results will tell them at a raw level. On this basis they will 'spec tables'. This means that they specify how they want the data tables to look.

In most cases each question will have one table, with the question printed out across the top with its question number and the table number. Down the left-hand side will be the multiple-choice answers or the open-ended answers, now reconstructed and allocated codes.

Tables for open-ended questions will look like this because the answers are grouped together:

1 Local/nearest/most convenient
2 On way to work/school/home
3 Cheapest/most special offers

A table for a pre-coded question will look like this down the left-hand side:

1 Tesco
2 Sainsbury
3 Marks and Spencer

Each question is usually analysed or cross-tabbed against the demographics. Each different sequence of cross-tabs is called a 'break'. A typical break would always start at the far left with a total column, and then might include a column for each of these:

1 Total	5 AB	9 Regular users
2 Females 15–34	6 C1	10 Light users
3 Females 35–54	7 C2	11 North
4 Females 55+	8 DE	12 South

Socio-economic groups

The columns headed AB, C1, C2, DE relate to socio-economic group. This topic is beyond the scope of this book, but you need to know that they are defined as follows:

A – Top management, professionals, top civil servants

B – Middle management, managers of small businesses

C1 – Junior management, owners of small establishments

C2 – Skilled manual workers

D – Semi-skilled and unskilled manual workers

E – Unemployed and on state benefit

Demographic classifications

It is the head of the household whose occupation determines the classification for their dependants. (Retired people are classified by the job they did before they retired.) Whether it is a man or woman, the person with the most senior or well-paid job is recorded as head of household. This is a hotly debated topic! In some countries the classification is based instead on the age the respondent finished full-time education. In order to code socio-economic group, a number of questions will have been asked about level of seniority, number of employees, size of business, etc.

Depending on the size and nature of the survey, there might be a regional north/south split or a split by TV region, sales region or administrative region.

The breaks across the top of the tables will be segments or types of consumers whose responses you particularly want to study. They can be formed of combinations of classifications such as 'females aged 25–34 who are regular users of the product'. Life stages are also popular breaks, for example 'single/no children, married no children, married with children, empty nesters'. It all depends on your target market, potential target market or the type of product you are researching. It is possible to have two or even three tables for each question using different breaks, particularly if you want to look at one aspect in more detail. For example, you might want a geographical table with just the regions on it.

Another popular option is to use 'cross-breaks' which are when you analyse one question by another, for example from likelihood to purchase X to where they would purchase it.

Scoring

Tables show both raw numbers of responses and a column and sometimes a row percentage. You can thus see what percentage of, say, women aged 25–34 made a certain response (column percentage) and what percentage of those making that response were women aged 25–34 (row percentage). Tables might also show a weighted percentage if a sub-sample of the population surveyed was artificially boosted to increase the statistical validity of the data.

Tables show the **base figure**, which is the total number of respondents on whom that table is based. This will usually be the number who answered that question. It is unwise, when analysing tables, to spec a table with a base of less than 100 respondents because the difference between percentages will not be statistically significant.

Tables covering the response to **Likert scales** will also show a mean score. Likert scales require the respondent to state their level of agreement with attitude statements, with 1 representing 'disagree strongly' and 5 representing 'agree strongly'. When analysing responses to each attitude statement, we often want to see the mean or average level of agreement or disagreement. Another option is to have scores 1 and 2 combined to show those who disagree slightly or strongly and 4 and 5 combined to show those who agree slightly or strongly.

The data-processing agency handling the data calculates how valid the data is, based on sample size, number answering the questions and range of answers given. This is called **significance testing** and addresses the issue of whether the results could have occurred by chance or whether they show a meaningful response that can only have occurred for that group of people. In other words, is this percentage difference important enough to be a factor in the marketing decision that will be based on it?

Statistical significance testing

Imagine you are testing four different pack designs. Pack A is preferred by 60% of the sample and Pack B by 40% of the sample. If only 50 people were asked, we'd be making a choice between 30 people preferring one and 20 preferring the other, which is not very reassuring. However, if there were 1,000 people in the sample, the difference would be between 600 and 400, which one could rely on with more confidence.

Statistical significance testing is how the computer works out all the figures and shows at the foot of each column of data the level of significance. This is a way to warn researchers off making big decisions based on scanty evidence. It is usually expressed as + or − x%.

Qualitative analysis

Depth interviews and focus groups are almost always recorded and then transcribed. The transcriptions show who said what, and also include responses such as '(laughter)' or '(all agreeing)' if the transcriber hears everyone saying 'yes' or 'I agree'. The transcript also indicates the points at which new stimuli are introduced. Any parts that the transcriber can't hear clearly are noted as '...' so that the researcher can check the recording themselves, or may remember what was said and can write it in. Sometimes a note taker attends the focus groups, and research projects with fast turnarounds may be reported from these notes.

Whereas analysis of quantitative research starts after fieldwork has finished, analysis of qualitative data is ongoing from the moment fieldwork starts. Qualitative researchers modify their questioning constantly in response to feedback from the group or interview, and they take that feedback on to their next group and the next as they gain understanding and insight. They are in a continual hypothesis-generating state, and this continues on through analysis and interpretation. Indeed, many qualitative debriefs or presentations are managed as brainstorming sessions or workshops to continue the exploratory process.

TIP

When analysing focus groups and depths, keep different samples separate so that you can understand each and compare them.

Although the differences between samples will have no statistical significance because the sample size is so small, differences do emerge and these may later be verified with a quantitative survey. In qualitative research the focus is on insight, understanding and exploration rather than facts and figures. The researcher is using their own intuition, experience and knowledge of psychology to analyse the data, whereas in quantitative research the analysis is done by a computer and is objective. For this reason qualitative research tends to be purchased on the basis that a client believes a particular researcher has the gift of understanding what respondents say and being able to interpret what they mean and its significance for them, the client, in terms of informing marketing decision making.

Qualitative researchers will use various different methods to analyse their transcripts including mind maps, diagrams, visual representations and computer software.

Summary

Today you learned that quantitative research begins on receipt of all the completed questionnaires, when the responses are translated into codes a computer can work with. These codes are then interrogated in various different ways to produce sets of tables displaying numbers and percentages. These are the result of cross-analysing the responses by demographics or other criteria, in order to make an objective assessment of the results.

By comparison, in qualitative research the analysis stage starts with the first depth interview or focus group and continues through to the presentation of results. It is an iterative process throughout the fieldwork. The analysis is subjective and based on the qualitative researcher's skills and experience of research, the product category and the sample.

While tables and other research results can make fascinating reading, they still need to be interpreted and expressed in a way that shows patterns clearly. You will learn about presenting results tomorrow.

Fact-check (answers at the back)

1. What are the three stages of analysis of quantitative research?
   a) Transcripts, coding, interpretation ❑
   b) Coding, data entry, tables ❑
   c) Data entry, significance testing, cross-breaks ❑
   d) Breaks, tables, mean score ❑

2. What social grouping would you record for a plumber?
   a) B ❑
   b) C1 ❑
   c) C2 ❑
   d) D ❑

3. How do you record the socio-economic group of a retired person?
   a) According to what job they had before they retired ❑
   b) E ❑
   c) According to what part-time work they have now ❑
   d) According to the pension they have ❑

4. Why do you need contact details of the respondent on the questionnaire?
   a) To check that the interview has genuinely taken place ❑
   b) To ask them more questions ❑
   c) To invite them to a focus group ❑
   d) To record their region for analysis ❑

5. What do coders do first with the responses from open-ended questions?
   a) Read them and try and understand what they mean ❑
   b) Enter them into the computer ❑
   c) Phone the respondent and ask them what they meant ❑
   d) List them and allocate numeric codes to the most popular answers ❑

6. What is data cleaning?
   a) Making sure every answer has a code ❑
   b) Using a red pen to circle the code ❑
   c) Checking for inconsistencies and missed questions ❑
   d) Removing dirty marks from the paper ❑

7. What is a hole count?
   a) Data tables with just the number of respondents who gave each possible answer to a question ❑
   b) The total number of holes in the questionnaire ❑
   c) The number of people in the sample ❑
   d) The number of interviews done per day ❑

8. Why is statistical significance important?
a) To avoid jumping to conclusions ❏
b) To impress the clients at the presentation ❏
c) To be confident that the difference between two percentages could not have happened just by chance ❏
d) Because the sample may be too small to draw meaningful conclusions ❏

9. How many different cross-breaks can you have on your data tables?
a) Ten ❏
b) One ❏
c) Two ❏
d) As many as you need ❏

10. What is a transcript?
a) The written record of what took place during a depth interview or focus group ❏
b) What the moderator remembers about the depth interview or focus group ❏
c) The recording of the depth interview or focus group ❏
d) The recording of the depth interview or focus group written down word for word ❏

SATURDAY

Report writing and presentation skills

Today we will look at how to turn data tables and qualitative data into a report and presentation so that they can fulfil their role as an information tool for marketing.

Your first task is to look back at the research brief and proposal, to reacquaint yourself with the marketing and research objectives. It can be tempting to become embroiled in the minutiae of all the process elements of running the survey and lose sight of the decisions that need to be taken based on the results.

What reporting and presentation requirement has been agreed in the proposal? Most research projects are now presented as a debrief using a PowerPoint presentation and sometimes, but not always, followed up with a detailed report. Because decisions need to be taken quickly, as soon as results are available, the detailed report may often be used as a reference document to be filed or used in the research department for building information about the brand.

The debrief presentation

A top-line debrief is arranged when decisions need to be taken in advance of the full research findings being known. This could be, for example, in a situation where qualitative research has taken place around new product development and the creative agency needs to know which concepts to develop for the next stage of research, but does not need the full detailed findings to set that in motion.

It would be easy to write a report or presentation by simply doing a PowerPoint slide or section of the report based on the structure of the questionnaire and then taking the audience or reader through it question by question. However, this is not the best way to do it for three reasons.

- The questionnaire is designed with the respondent in mind, to keep their interest, and not the marketing team.
- The questionnaire may use several questions to build up an understanding of, for example, the buying process or brand image, where they would more sensibly be combined for the marketing team who want to use the information.
- Even in quantitative surveys it is not so much the answers to the questions that are important but what the answers mean in the context of the marketing objectives.

The best approach is to use the standard presentation technique.

1 Tell them what you are going to tell them

Since people are busy and meetings are taking place all the time, it is a good idea to remind your audience of the subject of this presentation, the objectives that were set and what the research was conducted to provide. Simple slides for this are needed:

1 Project title and who you are, including contact details
2 Background – the background to the research, why it is being done now, what and who prompted it
3 Marketing objectives (verbatim from proposal)
4 Research objectives (verbatim from proposal)
5 Method and sample (basics – detail in report)

2 Tell them

Break down the findings into sections that tie in with the research objectives. In quantitative research presentations you will have summary tables and charts to communicate the findings visually. In qualitative research, you can expect video clips from the focus groups. (Unless you specifically request it, these will not be edited.)

3 Tell them what you've told them

Show a few slides of conclusions or main points that, expanded slightly, will also form the basis of your management or executive summary in the report.

4 Tell them what they should do next

A presentation or report should usually end with a section of recommendations, but this depends on the relationship with the client, whether the client is internal or external and what has previously been offered in the proposal. Whether specifically requested or not, it is a good discipline to imagine you have to do this because it ensures that you have provided all that is needed to be able to present this recommendation stage.

It is usual to allow time for questions at the end of the debrief. Stimuli are then returned and, if copies of the tables or DVDs of the focus groups have been requested, these will be handed over then. Remember that clients cannot have these unless respondents have signed a permission form at the start of the focus group.

Presentation skills

Your presentation gives you an opportunity to impress senior management at the client company, and ultimately it may affect whether you get another project from them. Get the most from it by using these key skills.

- Introduce yourself briefly. You want them to remember who you are. Give everyone your business card.
- Speak slowly, clearly and with inflection. There is nothing quite so soporific as a monotonous voice.
- Use eye contact to include everyone, and smile.
- Do not read from the screen or slide.
- Use a mixture of slide layouts.
- Use a variety of different types of charts, and use colour.
- Keep to time and ideally stay under it.

The research report

Clients do not always require a fully detailed research report and may be satisfied just with the debrief presentation. It will depend on the client and the nature of the survey. This will have been agreed at the briefing stage and will be recorded in the brief and proposal.

The report should usually contain:

1 Title page
2 Contents
3 Executive summary
4 Background
5 Research objectives
6 Method and sample
7 Research findings
8 Conclusions
9 Recommendations
10 Appendices

1 Title page

This should state:

● the name of the project given by the client
● the reference number they have allocated to it
● the completion date
● the name and contact details of the research agency
● the lead researcher and their direct contact details.

2 Contents

Make it easy for readers of your report to find the information they need quickly, with page numbers and clearly marked sections relating to the research objectives.

3 Executive summary

It is usual to include an executive summary in addition to, or as part of, the main report because this is usually the only section read by senior management. It should contain a brief note of the background, research and marketing objectives, methodology and key findings. Whether it also includes the recommendations will depend on the research proposal and agreement between client and agency.

4 Background

This can usually be taken straight from the research proposal. It needs to be included for two reasons.

- Some readers not directly involved in the research may not have read the proposal.
- The report may be read some time after the research by someone wanting to replicate the study, so they will want to read the background to the research at the time it was conducted.

5 Research objectives

This section will also mirror the research proposal and needs to be included for the same reason as the background.

6 Method and sample

Although this section will echo the methodology section of the proposal, it should specify how many interviews or focus groups were conducted, the sampling points (locations) and any experiences of the methodology that are pertinent and could potentially skew the findings. These should be noted in particular if the research or sample is to be replicated because of, for example, difficulties in recruiting specific target consumers or the length of the questionnaire.

The questionnaire or topic guide should be included in an appendix, but include a brief summary of each here.

7 Research findings

Divide this section according to the research objectives. Cover each product, design, commercial or whatever is being researched on a separate page. Include a summary page for comparisons across the sample. This works well for quantitative research, but for qualitative – especially exploratory – it may make more sense to separate different target groups so that readers can see each group in one place.

The findings should ideally tell the reader a story, so that the findings unfold and lead naturally to the next section, the conclusions. In this way you take the reader with you so that the conclusions 'fall out' of the findings in an obvious way.

Avoid using the questionnaire or discussion guide to structure this section. They were geared towards the respondent and don't necessarily reflect the needs of your readers, who want to tie in the findings with the objectives of the research and the marketing decisions they will need to make as a result.

8 Conclusions

These should be numbered and, again, related to the research objectives. One or two pages should suffice because here you are simply summarizing; readers can refer back to the findings for the detail.

9 Recommendations

By now, the recommendations should also be obvious to the reader if you have made a good job of writing the report. Again, number your points, which need cover no more than one page.

In the case of qualitative research recommendations, you may be suggesting quantification of some of the hypotheses generated by your conclusions. Quantitative research – especially ongoing continuous research, tracking research, usage and attitude surveys and research designed to inform – may not require recommendations, so ask the client whether you should include them.

10 Appendices

Include the following as appendices:

- a copy of the research brief
- the questionnaire or topic guide
- photographs of the stimuli
- tables.

General writing tips

- Use short, jargon-free sentences.
- Increase ease of use with bullet points.
- Include quotes, tables and charts.
- Use short paragraphs and bite-size chunks.
- Print the executive summary on different-coloured paper so it can easily be found.

Using the research

Market research is an ongoing process and each research presentation or report increases the fund of information for your organization or client. Once this project has been completed, consider whether other parts of the organization may benefit from any of the information and pass it on.

Summary

The final stage of a market research survey is the presentation, often called the debrief, and the report, if one is required. This is an opportunity to demonstrate your research skills and communicate effectively the findings of the research to your audience.

Today you learned that the structure of both presentation and report is crucial. They need to follow the lines set out in the proposal so that those less familiar with the project can easily follow the logic and see how to implement the findings. You need to take them on a journey through the project from the background – the hypothesis or problem the research was designed to address – through to its resolution in your conclusions and recommendations.

To prevent anything getting in the way of this process, use short punchy points and back them up with clear evidence. Don't use research jargon and maintain rapport through eye contact and humour. Avoid reading out the slides; instead, talk about the points on them and above all, make your presentation an enjoyable and informative experience.

Fact-check (answers at the back)

1. Why should you not use the questionnaire or discussion guide as the structure for your presentation or report?
   a) Because it's very long ☐
   b) Because it's designed with the respondents in mind ☐
   c) Because it doesn't make sense to marketing ☐
   d) Because your audience is not familiar with questionnaires ☐

2. When might you need a top-line presentation?
   a) When the client needs to make a decision quickly ☐
   b) When clients don't want a full presentation ☐
   c) When you don't have time to give a full presentation ☐
   d) When the research budget is small ☐

3. Which part of the report do you copy from the proposal?
   a) Research findings ☐
   b) Conclusions ☐
   c) Research objectives ☐
   d) Method ☐

4. What needs to go in the executive summary?
   a) The research findings ☐
   b) The conclusions ☐
   c) Recommendations ☐
   d) A summary of the report ☐

5. What should be in the appendices?
   a) Copies of the questionnaire ☐
   b) Copy of the discussion guide ☐
   c) Stimuli ☐
   d) All of the above ☐

6. Should you include recommendations in the report?
   a) Yes, always ☐
   b) Yes, if the client has asked you to ☐
   c) Never ☐
   d) If they are favourable to the client ☐

7. What needs to be added to the methodology section in the report?
   a) Anything that may affect interpretation of the findings ☐
   b) How the research was done ☐
   c) How many focus groups there were ☐
   d) How many interviews took place ☐

8. What needs to be included in the sample section?
   a) The questionnaire ☐
   b) The length of the interview ☐
   c) The number and location of interviews ☐
   d) The discussion guide ☐

9. Why should you avoid jargon?
   a) No one will understand it ☐
   b) It gets in the way of ease of understanding ☐
   c) It doesn't impress anyone ☐
   d) You may get it wrong ☐

10. What needs to be on the title page?
    a) Title and reference number of the survey ☐
    b) Your home telephone number ☐
    c) A photo of the product you are researching ☐
    d) The date fieldwork started ☐

116

Surviving in tough times

In tough times it's more important than ever for our market research to be as effective as possible. This book will teach you how to commission the market research that will enable you to get ahead of the competition by understanding your consumers and the market in which you operate. If you are looking to get into market research as a profession, reading it will give you enough basic information to impress any prospective employer and set you apart from others competing for the job. Here are ten crucial tips that you can use to enhance your market research skills.

1 Read the book: learn what market research is all about!

Market research is the key to understanding your consumers and customers in today's highly competitive market. Yes, it is expensive, but making the wrong decision or making a decision without the evidence for it can be much more costly. Market research is an investment in the future success of your company. This book shows you how to design research that will provide the information you need to make confident marketing decisions.

2 Do your own market research

Even with no budget you can research your competition. You can do this by visiting stores, looking at competitor websites, talking to consumers, friends and colleagues and identifying the key factors that play a part in decision making for your product or service. Find out about changes in attitudes and usage as a result of the changing economic environment. Don't be shy: ask away!

3 Use what's there already

You can find research reports in libraries, in trade magazines, via trade organizations and in newspapers. The Chartered Institute of Marketing holds copies of market research reports and industry studies. For the cost of membership you can have easy access to more information than you can imagine.

4 Study your sales figures

There's so much information already stored within your own data in your organization. Use it to look for patterns in your sales data, so that you become more alert to changes in demand. What prompted rises in sales? What pre-empted the falls in sales? What could you do differently as a result?

5 Use your customers as a resource

Talk to your key customers. Use the questionnaire design skills you have learned this week to design your own questionnaire and send it to your key customers with an encouraging covering letter. This will help you keep information on customers up to date, so that you can identify the right course of action to meet your objectives in a changing environment.

Give your customers some feedback afterwards to tell them what you've learned and how you will use the information they've given you.

6 Use Google

During difficult times, customers may be changing in terms of their perceived needs, buying habits and attitudes to value. Don't assume you know what your customers are thinking. By doing a search for mentions of your brand, product or service, you can learn a great deal about how people talk about your brand and who they are, what your brand means to them and what you could do to improve the consumer connection.

7 Brainstorm

Run a brainstorming session with your colleagues and customers to explore how you could improve what you do to steal a march on the competition. Use them as a resource. Brainstorming enables people to express unstructured, unrelated ideas in a way that prompts great ideas. Collect these ideas and use them to help inform your marketing decisions.

8 Look at past research reports and tables

Research is done for a specific purpose but within these reports you'll find ideas that could be useful today. They may not have been relevant when the research was done but they may be now. Look among the 'other ideas' for inspiration. This can help to make you more creative in your response to changing economic conditions.

9 Use recruitment interviews as a resource

When interviewing potential employees, ask them what they would do and what ideas they have. They will have researched your company and your products or services to prepare themselves for the interview, and so they will have fresh ideas. Allow these ideas to challenge you and lead you to fresh ways of thinking.

10 Use social media

You can do market research using your Facebook, Twitter and LinkedIn groups. Use the principles described in the book to design effective questions and analyse them to present to your colleagues. This is an efficient way of keeping up to date with your market to ensure that you select the right strategic responses to the current situation. Feed back to your social media the actions you have taken as a result of your research.

Glossary

Back-check – email or phone call made to a respondent to check that the interview has taken place and one or two questions asked to check validity of responses.

CAPI (computer-assisted personal interview) – personal interviewing using a laptop in place of paper-based questionnaires

CATI (computer-assisted telephone interview) – interviews completed on the phone

Closed questions – questions that have a given list of possible responses (called **pre-codes**) to choose from, which the interviewer records

Fieldwork – the stage of the survey that involves interviewing

Hall test – a central location such as a church hall or community centre with access to high traffic of shoppers or the target consumers, e.g. a university bar. Interviewers invite respondents into the venue and administer a questionnaire

Hit rate – percentage of the public likely to qualify for interview, according to the quota set based on the supplier's proposal

Incentive – payment, in cash or in kind, made to the respondent as a 'thank you' for taking part in the interview

Interviewer – a trained person administering the questionnaire according to given instructions and abiding by the Market Research Code of Conduct

Moderator – a trained person guiding the focus group using a topic guide and projective techniques to elicit consumer response to stimulus material such as concept boards

Open (or open-ended) questions – questions the respondent can answer in their own words, which are then recorded or written down by the interviewer

Probing – delving deeper beyond an initial answer by asking 'In what way?', 'How do you do that?' or, 'Tell me more about...'

Projective techniques – indirect questioning to encourage a less rationalized response to stimulus, e.g. 'What words come to mind when I say "ketchup"?' or the use of collage and mood boards to stimulate discussion, role play, thematic apperception tests, etc.

Prompting – reminding the respondent about something they've said earlier, e.g. 'You said earlier that...' or asking them to continue by saying, 'What else?' or, 'What other reasons?'

Quota – the number of interviews that need to be done in each age/social class/usage category, e.g. 5 × 25–34-year-old males

Recruiter – an interviewer trained to recruit respondents to depth interviews or focus groups

Recruitment questionnaire/screener – short questionnaire to elicit whether the respondent corresponds to the profile set out in the research proposal in terms of the recruitment criteria

Respondent – the person being interviewed

Sampling point – location where a number of interviews take place to represent the area overall

Show cards – set of cards showing multiple-choice answers and any pictures that need to be shown. The interviewer has a set to avoid having to show the respondent the questionnaire; she hands the respondent the show cards instead

Skew – where the data is not representative of 'the universe' because of the way the question has been asked, in terms of respondent or area selection, type of questionnaire used, etc.

Stimulus material – whatever is being shown to respondents, e.g. concept boards, mood boards, mocked-up product, pilot episodes of a TV show, pilot commercial

Thematic apperception test – a bubble cartoon that the respondent completes. It transposes the respondent's feeling to the person in the cartoon

Viewing studio – a collection of rooms set up as a lounge or meeting room with a one-way mirror and room behind. Clients can sit and watch the group or interview without being seen, although respondents must be told this is happening. The images from this viewing studio can be transmitted via the Internet, enabling clients all over the world to watch the group and input their comments to each other and to the moderator

Bibliography

Bartkowiak, Judy, *Secrets of Success in Brand Licensing*, 1st edition (London: MX Publishing, 2011)

Bradley, Nigel, *Marketing Research*, 2nd edition (Oxford: Oxford University Press, 2010)

Wilson, Alan, *Marketing Research – An Integrated Approach*, 3rd edition (Harlow: FT Prentice Hall, 2012)

Answers

Sunday: 1c; 2b; 3a; 4c; 5b; 6a; 7c; 8c; 9d; 10a.

Monday: 1d; 2b; 3c; 4a; 5d; 6b; 7c; 8d; 9c; 10d.

Tuesday: 1c; 2d; 3a; 4b; 5d; 6a; 7b; 8c; 9d; 10b.

Wednesday: 1d; 2a; 3b; 4c; 5a; 6d; 7b; 8b; 9d; 10a.

Thursday: 1c; 2a; 3d; 4a; 5b; 6d; 7d; 8a; 9b; 10b.

Friday: 1b; 2c; 3a; 4a; 5d; 6c; 7a; 8c; 9d; 10d.

Saturday: 1b; 2a; 3c; 4d; 5d; 6b; 7a; 8c; 9b; 10a.